Promoting Gc

Principles, Practic

Published by: Commonwealth Secretariat
                     Marlborough House
                     Pall Mall
                     London SW1Y 5HX
                     UNITED KINGDOM

Copyright   ©   Commonwealth Secretariat

May be purchased from:

Publications Unit
Commonwealth Secretariat

Telephone: +44 (0) 20 7747 6342
Facsimile: +44 (0) 20 7839 9081

ISBN: 0 85092 629 7

Price: £9.00/$14.00

Promoting Good Governance

Principles, Practices and Perspectives

Commonwealth Secretariat
2000

FOREWORD

A strong and achieving public service is a necessary condition for a competitively successful nation. The Management and Training Services Division (MTSD) of the Commonwealth Secretariat assists member governments to improve the performance of the public service through action-oriented advisory services, policy analysis and training. This assistance is supported by funds from the Commonwealth Fund for Technical Co-operation (CFTC).

Commonwealth co-operation in public administration is facilitated immeasurably by the strong similarities that exist between all Commonwealth countries in relation to the institutional landscape and the underlying principles and values of a neutral public service. In mapping current and emerging best practices in public service management, MTSD has been able to draw on the most determined, experienced and successful practitioners, managers, and policy-makers across the Commonwealth. Their experiences point the way to practical strategies for improvement.

The concept of good governance is very much interlinked with institutionalised values such as democracy, observance of human rights, accountability, transparency and greater efficiency and effectiveness of the public sector. Public management, as a discipline, presents certain techniques strategies and methods intended to improve the public service reform process and, more importantly, to enable the machinery of government to be cost-conscious and performance-oriented.

This publication focuses on key elements of good governance with particular emphasis on the public sector and related issues, practices, principles and perspectives. It therefore discusses the role of public management in promoting productivity and increasing performance in the pursuit of efficiency, effectiveness, economic growth, sustainable development and social justice. The public/private sector interface is discussed in the context of developing a meaningful and effective partnership in economic development.

Michael Gillibrand
Acting Director and Special Adviser
Management and Training Services Division.

CONTENTS

ACKNOWLEDGEMENTS

The Commonwealth Secretariat is grateful to Sam Agere, Special Adviser (Management Development) in the Management and Training Services Division, who authored and edited this publication. Special thanks are due to the following persons whose contributions, advice and assistance have contributed to the success of this publication:

Professor Ladipo Adamolekun, Principal Public Management Specialist in the World Bank, for the use of much of the material he presented at the UNDP/World Bank-sponsored workshop for Heads of the Civil Service in Africa, held in Windhoek, Namibia; Dr Ijuka Kabumba, Secretary-General of the African Association for Public Administration and Management, for permission to use some of the conference papers presented at the 1998 Roundtable Conference by Professor Kwame Frimpong, Professor of Law at the University of Botswana, and Dr Asemelash Beyeni of Economic Commission for Africa, Addis Ababa, Ethiopia; and Mr Gordon Draper, Professor of Public Administration at the University of West Indies and former Minister of Public Administration and Information in the Government of Trinidad and Tobago (Caribbean), for his contribution on the implications for teaching and training in management.

Thanks are also due to Roy Chalmers, Greg Covington and Mrs Ivy Chikoti for their assistance in the production of this publication.

Although in editing, every attempt has been made to retain the accuracy of the contributions, the final responsibility for any errors or inaccuracies rests with the Commonwealth Secretariat.

CONCEPTS AND ISSUES

INTRODUCTION

Good governance is a concept that has recently come into regular use in political science, public administration and, more particularly, development management. It appears alongside such concepts and terms as democracy, civil society, popular participation, human rights and social and sustainable development. In the last decade, it has been closely associated with public sector reform. Within the public management discipline or profession it has been regarded as an aspect of the New Paradigm in Public Administration which emphasises the role of public managers in providing high quality services that citizens value; advocates increasing managerial autonomy, particularly by reducing central agency controls; demands, measures and rewards both organisational and individual performance; recognises the importance of providing the human and technological resources that managers require to meet their performance targets; and is receptive to competition and open-minded about which public purposes should be performed by public servants as opposed to the private sector.[1]

A number of important perspectives emerge from this new paradigm, which has been the focus of debate in the political arena as well as in academic institutions. The emerging perspectives regarding governance structures are:

- the relationship between governments and the markets;
- the relationship between governments and citizens;
- the relationship between governments and the voluntary or private sector;
- the relationship between elected (politicians) and appointed (civil servants);
- the relationship between local government institutions and urban and rural dwellers;
- the relationship between legislature and the executive; and
- the relationship between nation states and international institutions.

In analysing these perspectives, many public management practitioners and theoreticians from academic institutions and institutes of public administration have formulated various procedures and processes through which genuine good governance can be achieved and have identified the principles and assumptions that underpin good governance. The practitioners have also drawn on examples of best practice for use in putting the concept into practice. Different

perspectives, principles and best practices have been the subject of debate at many national and international conferences attempting to define good governance.

The Prime Minister of Malaysia, Dr Mahathir Mohamed, defined good governance as the exercise of political, economic and administrative authority to manage a nation's affairs. This includes the complex array of mechanisms, processes, relationships and institutions through which citizens manage affairs involving public life.[2] He further stated that current conditions show that governance is no longer the exclusive domain of the state. Various bodies, almost self-appointed, now claim a right to have a role in the governance of a country. The Ministerial Symposium of the Organisation for Economic Co-operation and Development (OECD) on the future of the Public Service, held in Paris, March 1996, defined good governance in terms of relationships. This covers more than public administration and the relationships, methods and instruments of relationships between government and citizens, acting both as individuals and as part of institutions, e.g. political parties, productive enterprises, special interest groups and the media.[3]

The symposium regarded the quality and effectiveness of governance as crucial to national prosperity. As a concept, governance goes beyond the issue of public management to the more fundamental question of how, in a modern society, democracy can be adapted to help countries resolve the problems they face.

Defined in this manner, the concept has different implications for stakeholders such as the state, civil society and public administration institutions. The institutions of public administration, for example, would have to identify their role within the parameters of a dynamic society. However, it appears that the primary focus for such institutions is to include key relationships and systems of decision-making and accountability. As training institutions, they are interested not only in the effectiveness of such institutions but also in their integrity and the types of values that they embody. They would ensure that the government maintains the public service in a good state and hands it over, undamaged, to its successor at the end of its term.

Donor and or multilateral agencies have taken a leading role in defining good governance. Corkery states that since 1989, governance has taken on a much wider range of geographical spread and meaning. Even in the development co-operation field, this variation of meaning has been evident. The World Bank provides some indications of the various contexts in which the term governance began to be used. In its first report, explicitly on the theme of governance and development (1992), it defined governance as a way in which power is exercised in the management of the economic and social resources of a country, notably with a view to development. It underlined three aspects in governance:

1. type of political regime;
2. process by which authority is exercised in the management of economic and social resources, with a view to development; and
3. capacity of governments to formulate policies and have them effectively implemented[4]

The following years saw many bilateral and multilateral agencies defining good governance. The 1993 report of the African Development Bank made use of the term at the macro, mezzo and micro-economic levels. The Inter-American Bank emphasised the modernisation of public administration in the context of governance. The Overseas Development Administration (now Department for International Development, (DFID)) in the United Kingdom emphasised the normative aspect of good governance. It took account of political, economic and administrative dimensions of governance to develop criteria, thus facilitating use of governance as a guide in the allocation of aid. The Aid to Development Commission of Organisation for Economic Co-operation and Development (OECD) used the World Bank's definition and linked it to participatory development, human rights and democratisation (the legitimacy of government and policy arms of governments, and transparency of decision-making).[5]

The Commonwealth has shown its commitment to good governance through declarations made by Heads of State at their biennial meetings. The 1991 Harare Commonwealth declaration, for example, committed members to the democratic process and institutions which reflect national circumstances, the rule of law and the independence of the judiciary, just and honest government, fundamental human rights, including equal rights and opportunities for all citizens, regardless of race, colour, creed or political belief.[6]

The United Nations Development Programme (UNDP) defined good governance more or less as above but placed greater emphasis on sustainable human development (UN Report, 1998). Clearly, the definition varies from one organisation to the other, although general ideas and focus on issues are the same. As has been observed through the definitions above, the World Bank puts emphasis on economic and social resources for development, the OECD emphasises human rights, democracy and legitimacy of government. UNDP emphasises human development, the elimination of poverty, and public administration. It has even established a Management and Governance Division.

The discretionary space left by the lack of a clear, well-defined scope for what governance encompasses allowed users to choose and set their own parameters. Because of these gaps in the definition of the concept, Western creditor governments and international financial institutions reinforced pressures for reforms in a number of developing countries. From the 1980s, they began to impose stringent economic conditions on the provision of debt relief and new loans. They then widened conditionality to include transparent administration, the protection of human rights, the restoration of democracy and the reform of the public service.

The World Bank also made issues of corruption a major element in its governance agenda. Aside from greater internal scrutiny of staff practices to ensure that they abide by high ethical standards, the use of World Bank resources by client countries was being closely monitored to ensure probity and integrity. Supported by the Global Coalition for Africa, anti-corruption activities are now central to the many World Bank country programmes. In instances where there is:

(a)   full agreement between World Bank and client country; and

(b)   the Bank has the capacity to enforce codes of conduct, sound procurement and audit recommendations,

an agreement is signed between them expressing a commitment to pursue anti-corruption. Providers of goods and services bidding on contracts also have to sign an anti-corruption pledge specifically stating that sanctions are accepted where bribes are given or offered to government officials.

GOOD GOVERNANCE: MEANS OR ENDS

We have discussed various definitions and interpretations of the concept of good governance. However, the rationale for the development of the concept in the last decade also varies between organisations whose focus is related to their broad goals and mandates.

As indicated here, good governance is used both as a means and as an end in itself. It becomes an end in itself if it addresses all its major elements satisfactorily. This implies that society is generally satisfied with the procedures and processes of arriving at solutions to problems, even if they may not necessarily agree on the methods and conclusions. Good governance is therefore the highest state of development and management of a nation's affairs. It is good that a democratic form of government is in place, that people participate in decision-making processes, that services are delivered efficiently, that human rights are respected, and that the government is transparent, accountable and productive.

The concept can also be regarded as a means to an end in that, in general, it contributes to economic growth, human development and social justice. Good governance as a concept will be used in this context of the public service reform or new public management paradigm. Within administrative reform it is used as a means of addressing other contemporary issues such as institutional development, capacity-building, decentralisation of power and authority, relations between politicians and appointed officials, co-ordination and the roles that heads of government play in promoting good governance. Good governance can be attained by identifying the following characteristics and practices of poor governance:

- failure to make a clear distinction between what is public and private, hence a tendency to divert public resources for private gain;
- failure to establish a predictable framework of law, government behaviour and the rule of law;
- excessive rules and regulations which impede the functioning of markets;
- priorities inconsistent with development, resulting in a misallocation of resources;
- excessively narrow-based or non-transparent decision-making processes;
- lack of a code of conduct in managing the affairs of the state;
- lack of clearly defined policy assumptions.

The absence of good governance has proved to be particularly damaging to the corrective intervention role of government. Programmes of poverty alleviation and environmental protection, for example, can be totally undermined by a lack of public accountability, corruption and the capture of public services by elites. Funds intended for the poor may be directed to the benefit of special interest groups, and the poor may have inadequate access to legal remedies.

Corruption tends to weaken the ability of governments to carry out their functions efficiently. Bribery and nepotism, for example, can cripple administration and dilute equity from the provision of government services and thus also determines social cohesiveness.

Good governance can also be conceptualised as part of a development process. The proper management of the public service, as an instrument of the state, is in itself a facilitator in development process. Public management as a discipline and a profession, therefore, contributes to the development process through the improvement of the management system, which delivers the service to the public.

Experience has shown that managing the public service is becoming increasingly complex, perhaps because public policy issues are becoming more international and involve stakeholders. The boundaries between policy formulation and management are becoming blurred as both managers and policy-makers are interlinked. The private sector and civil society are now playing a larger role in public affairs. In management, more and more responsibilities are delegated and devolved to managers, encouraging them to take risks whilst being accountable for their decisions. The managers are also caught up between new performance demands and traditional control systems. There is more emphasis in management capabilities, competencies and achieving set goals with limited resources. It is in the context of the various tasks, responsibilities and expectations that public management as an instrument for development is becoming more complex than ever before.

This development process is made more complex by features of managerial excellence in the public service which require that there should be a degree of commitment to values, placing a high priority on service to clients and citizens; dedication to the notion of public service; a participative approach to leadership; and a programmatic approach to change.

Considering these features of managerial excellence, public management is no longer seen as an independent activity but as being closely linked to economic performance and in the mainstream of political agendas. Global pressures to co-operate and compete, rising expectations of citizens, and the need to reduce public deficits are changing the way countries need to be governed. As a result of these internal and external pressures, governments have responded by undertaking public management reforms, which are not only considered as definitive solutions but also as a continuous development process.

At a theoretical and philosophical level, it appears that some public service reforms are based on the neo-liberal theory. One of the main postulates of the neo-liberal theory is deregulation. The theory assumes that the state should interfere as little as possible in economic affairs and should only manage what it can, leaving out what can be done best by other sectors or organisations and individuals.

Good governance is therefore, among other things, participatory, transparent and accountable, in order to ensure that political, social and economic priorities are based on a broad consensus in society, and that the voices of the poorest and most vulnerable are heard in the decision-making processes regarding the allocation of resources. Defined in this manner, good governance has major implications for equity, poverty and quality of life. Political governance is the process of decision-making to formulate policy. Administrative governance is the system of policy implementation. Encompassing all three, good governance defines the process and structures that guide political and socio-economic relationships.

KEY ELEMENTS OF GOOD GOVERNANCE

While there may be no best way of achieving good governance, the following stand out as the most common elements. These are accountability, transparency, combating corruption, participatory governance and an enabling legal/judicial framework.

Accountability

Accountability is defined as holding responsible elected or appointed individuals and organisations charged with a public mandate to account for specific actions, activities or decisions to the public from whom they derive their authority. In a narrow sense, accountability focuses on the ability to account for the allocation, use and control, i.e. budgeting, accounting, and auditing. In a broader sense, it is also concerned with the establishment and enforcement of rules and regulations of corporate governance.

Transparency

Transparency is broadly defined as public knowledge of the policies of government and confidence in its intentions. This requires making public accounts verifiable, providing for public participation in government policy-making and implementation, and allowing contestation over choices impacting on the lives of citizens. It also includes making available for public scrutiny accurate and timely information on economic and market conditions.

Combating Corruption

Corruption is defined as the abuse of public office or public trust for private gains. The definition covers most forms of corruption in both the public and private sectors. Combating corruption is a key indicator of commitment to good governance. Corruption can manifest itself as individual, organisational or institutional.

In the context of the state, corruption most often refers to criminal or otherwise unlawful conduct by government agencies, or by officials of these organisations acting in the course of their employment.

Poor governance and corruption are major constraints to the pursuit of economic development. For example:

- Bribery increases the costs of government development programmes and spawns projects of little economic merit.

- Corruption undermines revenue collection capacity, contributing to fiscal weaknesses and macro-economic difficulties.

- Diversion of resources from their intended purposes distorts the formulation of public policy.

- The use of bribes to gain access to public services undermines stated allocation priorities, benefiting the few at the expense of the many.

- Widespread corruption brings government into disrepute and encourages cynicism about politics and public policy.[7]

In public management, weaknesses in public administration result in a decline in the probity of public servants and inadequate legislative oversight of government. Further, corruption erodes the authority and effectiveness of public institutions. Improvements, therefore, in the effectiveness and transparency of economic policies and administrative reform can contribute powerfully to the fight against corruption a well as enhance good governance.

Stakeholder Participation

Participation is defined as a process whereby stockholders exercise influence over public policy decisions, and share control over resources and institutions that affect their lives, thereby providing a check on power of government. In the context of governance, participation is focused on the empowerment of citizens, including women and addressing the interplay between the broad range of civil societies, actors and actions. It is about the creation of an enabling regulatory framework and economic environment, which generates legitimate demands and monitors government policies and actions. It occurs at various levels: at the grassroots, through local and civic institutions; at the regional and national levels, through flexible and decentralised form of government; and also in the private sector.

Legal and Judicial Framework

A pro-governance and pro-development legal and judicial system is one in which laws are clear and are uniformly applied through an objective and independent judiciary. It is also one in which the legal system provides the necessary sanctions to deter or penalise breach. It promotes rule of law, human rights and private capital flows. In its absence or when it is weak, private capital flows may be discouraged, transaction costs are distorted, and rent-seeking activities become rampant. Enforcement involves firm action against corrupt behaviour at all levels.

The Links between Democracy and Elements of Good Governance

Accountability, transparency and reduction in the incidence of corruption are essential conditions for securing effectiveness in the use of public resources, promoting public welfare, enhancing governmental responsiveness and therefore enhancing the overall legitimacy of the political system.

An enabling legal and judicial framework fosters rule of law and respect for human as well as property rights. It is therefore a key condition for the creation of a stable economic environment and the stimulation of private sector development.

Stakeholder participation is crucial in engaging the energies and commitment of people for sustained development and in fostering equity of distribution of the benefits of development. Indeed, in the context of divided societies and gender inequality, inclusive civic participation and respect for human rights are

9

necessary for the generation of social capital and societal cohesion. It helps to foster trust and reciprocity between citizens and their governments, the state and private sector, and among different social and political groupings (ethnic, religious and regional) of the country. Respect for human rights promotes the enjoyment of the basic freedoms of expression, assembly and association, which empower citizens to act to improve their living conditions. It also makes it possible for civil society, the media and advocacy groups to criticise and demand redress from inefficient state policies.

Good governance, therefore, encompasses many of the essential elements of democracy such as participation, opening up to civil society, respect for human, civil and property rights, as well as peaceful conflict management. In common with democracy, good governance promotes the decentralisation of decision-making, implementation and monitoring. It also fosters the empowerment of civil society, the private sector and other key stakeholders.

Who are the major actors in promoting good governance?

There are three major institutions that promote good governance. These are the state, the private sector, and civil society. The successful interaction between them would ensure sustainable human development. Good governance therefore, encompasses effective states, mobilised civil society and a productive private sector. Good governance is facilitated by effective states that create enabling political and legal environments for economic growth and equitable distribution. It is dependent on vibrant civil societies, which mobilise groups and communities, facilitate political and social interaction, ensure participatory governance, help generate social capital, and foster social cohesion.

The World Bank states that good governance is central to creating and sustaining an environment, which fosters a strong and equitable development and is an essential component to sound economic policies. Governments play a key role in the provision of public goods. They establish the rules that make markets work efficiently and, more problematically, they correct for market failure. In order to play this role, they need revenues, and agents to collect revenues and produce the public goods. This, in turn, requires systems of accountability, adequate and reliable information, and efficiency in resource management and the delivery of public services.

The promotion of good governance therefore depends upon efficient public sector management, accountability, a legal framework for development, access to information, and transparency.

The reforms in public sector management are seen as part of good governance in that they focus on the overall management of resources for human development with special emphasis on accountability, institutional and legal framework for development and information and transparency. Public sector reforms also aim to create an enabling environment for growth. They, in addition, seek more efficient use of resources through the formulation of visions, a mission, strategic plans, and functional reviews, and by cutting fiscal deficits, reducing duplication and improving the delivery of service.

Improving Public Sector Management and Good Governance

When the capacity of the public sector to manage the economy and deliver public service is weak, the prospect for development is poor. The public sector in many developing countries has been characterised by uneven revenue collection, poor expenditure control and management of a bloated civil service, a large parastatal sector that provides poor returns on the scarce public funds invested in it, and weaknesses in the capacity of core economic agencies to design and implement policies that would address the problems.

Within the civil service, reforms and good governance can be achieved through the strengthening of personnel management and the effectiveness of public agencies. Poor fiscal management and inadequate government personnel policies (in areas such as recruitment, promotion and remuneration) result in a decline in the efficiency of the public sector. Improvements in economic and fiscal management, as well as in personnel management policies, are therefore key components of a strategy to enhance good governance.

Civil service reforms restore the morale and integrity of the public service through merit-based recruitment and promotion, and reduce the size and tasks of the administration to levels consistent with available fiscal resources, thereby making it easier to enhance emoluments and reward good performance.

Contemporary issues in promoting good governance

While the key elements of good governance have been discussed, there is a need to identify how widespread the issues are in a particular country or region. What may be a priority or a critical element in good governance in one country may not be regarded or accorded the same importance in another country. For example, the conduct of free and fair elections may be a priority in one country while the eradication of corruption may not be regarded as critically important in another.

In order to facilitate the identification, promotion and widespread coverage of the key elements in good governance and, more importantly, to find strategies for solutions, there may be a need to:

- Conduct seminars, debates and conferences in which the best practices are shared between and among government officials at both policy and programme levels.

- Identify emerging issues on the role of the state, private sector and civil society in service delivery. Discussion could focus on accountability of public servants to management and the public, incentives for improved performance and better quality services, and non-state provision of social services.

- Develop new guidelines and principles for new approaches to good governance and demonstrate some successes. Improve efficiency and the scope and quality of public service provision.

- Promote programmes that encourage forms of partnership between the public and private sector and civil society organisations in the delivery of service to the public.

- Assist governments with public sector reforms that facilitate the promotion of good governance and eradicate corruption.

- Persuade governments, through dialogue, of the need for institutional and public sector management assessments, respect for human rights and the rule of law.

- Help countries deal with especially complex issues of poverty alleviation and environment for which the quality of government performance is important.

Several keywords have been used to indicate what is expected of good governance: accountability, transparency and the goals of the economy. Efficiency and effectiveness are the requirements placed primarily on managers. Decentralisation, devolution, pluralism and the strengthening of

12

checks and balances focus more on structures for which responsibility rests with politicians. Participation, partnership, poverty alleviation, empowerment, ownership, human rights, free speech and free association and democracy require the active co-operation of all.

Good governance is, therefore, a wide subject area that ranges from:

- economic liberalism which constitutes private ownership, more investment and greater equality;

- political pluralism, which refers to participation of people in the development process, decentralisation of authority from the centre and democracy;

- social development which includes human rights rule of law, independent judiciary and free press;

- administrative accountability which refers to transparency, less corruption, economy, efficiency and effectiveness; and

- public sector reforms, strategic planning and management of change.

It is not possible to cover all these themes here. However, this publication aims to cover certain aspects of governance which have particular emphasis on the public sector reforms but which cut across each of the four themes mentioned above.

MANAGEMENT PROGRAMMES IN SUPPORT OF GOOD GOVERNANCE

In order to facilitate the promotion of good governance, to share examples of best practice with governments and to find appropriate conditions and solutions in different countries, some development agencies, and in particular the Commonwealth Secretariat, have been mounting programmes on policy and management development for member countries. These programmes have been conducted at Commonwealth, regional and individual country levels. Requests for such programmes have largely been driven by the needs and priorities of respective countries.

With technical assistance from the Commonwealth Fund for Technical Co-operation (CFTC), the Management and Training Services Division has been organising, at the requests of governments, policy and management development programmes in the following areas:

1. *Governance Structures and the Democratic Process*

The focus of this programme has been on the role of parliament and its relationship with the executive. The rationale for this focus was based on three factors: first, practically all Commonwealth countries have now embraced liberal democratic values, and their determination to guard these jealously has brought into greater focus the role of institutions such as parliament and oversight bodies in the consolidation of the democratic reforms; secondly, is the impact of on-going reforms in other sectors, notably the economy and public administration. A significant feature of these is the far-reaching change towards more open market-based economic arrangements and public administrative reform. Coupled with this, globalisation and recent phenomenal improvements in information technology have galvanised greater interdependence amongst states, making it increasingly impossible for any to survive without actively collaborating with others. By the same token, public sector management has responded to the need to limit the erstwhile role of the state and broaden the participation of civil society. The third important point is the role of the Commonwealth itself. The organisation – beginning with the 1991 Harare Commonwealth Declaration and continuing with subsequent declarations of the Heads of Government and activities of both the Secretariat and its affiliate bodies – and the Commonwealth Parliamentary Association (CPA), have striven to educate and support its members in dealing with the different dimensions of these developments.[8]

The objectives of this kind of interface are first to examine parliament-executive relations in the context of contemporary governance issues and challenges; secondly, to review selected Commonwealth experiences of the parliamentary oversight role and to draw general lessons; thirdly to develop guidelines on good practices for the responsibilities and management of parliamentary committees' interface with government; and fourthly, to assess the overall impact of parliament on the executive and make recommendations on strengthening its capacity to continue to perform its role.

2. *Strengthening Cabinet Decision-Making*

A few programmes have been mounted which focus on strengthening Cabinet as a machinery of the state. In most countries, the constitution provides the fundamental governance framework with which a society allocates and constrains the powers to govern in the public interest. It is a necessary but insufficient condition of good governance. Sufficiency comes from the Executive having effective means of ensuring that good decisions are taken and are executed in good time. The apex of that process is the Cabinet.

To assist systematic thinking about improving Cabinet performance, the focus of programmes has been on the basic functions of Cabinet, some typical deficiencies in the outputs of Cabinet activity and some of the institutional and process devices that have been employed in different countries to remedy those deficiencies.[9]

There are general principles of governance, which apply to any complex organisation. Most governments face the same, broadly similar problems to which they must find solutions. But when choices have to be made of possible solutions, the relevance and value of specific processes and techniques can be assessed only in the specific context of each country, taking account of the nature of that country's political and governmental institutions, the background against which these operate, their policy priorities and the different operational risks which they face.

3. The Political and Administrative Interface

The programmes to support the formal relationship between the Minister (elected official) and the Permanent Secretary (appointed official) are based on the assumption that successful policy development and management depends upon a meaningful relationship between the two sets of officials. The interface, or the working relationship between the politician and the civil servant, becomes critical to the success of administrative reforms.

The purpose of these programmes is to:

- identify emerging problems, issues and constraints facing the Minister and the Permanent Secretary in the management and reform of the public service;

- re-define the roles and responsibilities of the Minister and the permanent secretary in the implementation of the administrative reforms;

- identify policy and administrative boundaries between elected and appointed officials;

15

- identify the contributing factors to successful and unsuccessful patterns of interaction between politicians and public servants;

- share the best practices, processes and procedures of enhancing the functional relationship through the exchange of ideas and experiences.[10]

Such programmes have been conducted in all regions of the Commonwealth by the author in the Caribbean, Africa, Indian Ocean and the South Pacific and have been found to be useful in guiding the relationship towards fruitful ends.

4. Local governance and Institutional Development

Several management programmes have been organised to support and strengthen local government institutions and to build capacity to respond appropriately to the needs of the local people. The programmes have assisted governments in making choices when confronted with the need to re-organise administrative and political structures and procedures designed to decentralise government and administration. The programmes have been based on the assumption that well-functioning, self-sufficient local authorities can identify needs more accurately and mobilise people and resources on a sustained basis and are therefore better at implementing development strategies. A tremendous potential exists for local authorities to provide a full range of services in support of national economic development.[11]

Decentralisation is one of the areas of broad strategic choice relating to the structure of government. Administrative reform for decentralisation is intended to achieve both good management and good governance more generally. The programmes have emphasised the participation of people in decision-making and development at local level. Participation – or empowering – of local people is considered as both a precondition of decentralisation and an objective of it. This is because participation is itself a means to other ends, such as empowerment, the effective identification of local needs, the mobilisation of resources, and acceptance of change, etc.[12]

5. Support of Oversight Institutions

A lot of support has been provided to oversight institutions, such as the Ombudsman. The support has been mainly in the training and upgrading of staff skills and knowledge in the operation of their duties. Similar support has also been offered to the Electoral Commission, Judiciary, Comptroller and

Auditor-General's Office and the Anti-Corruption Commissions. The officials in these offices have been supported through grants to attend appropriate training courses, study visits and to create linkages between and among the countries themselves. Most Ombudsmen offices and Anti-Corruption Commissions in many of the Commonwealth developing countries have been weak in that they were not provided with the requisite staff with the right qualifications. In still other countries, there has been a lot of political interference, thereby threatening the autonomy of the organisation.

6. Anti-Corruption Measures

Commonwealth Finance Ministers, having identified some of the causes of corruption and its impact on the poor, government and public administration, made a number of suggestions and solutions. Anti-corruption measures were debated at a forum organised by the Commonwealth Secretariat. The Ministers recognised that the fight against corruption should go hand in hand with more general efforts to improve economic governance. Sustained action was required at two levels:

- systemic reforms which target the underlying weaknesses in policy, administration and politics and create an environment conducive to the elimination of corruption; and

- specific, focused, national anti-corruption strategies.

In mounting a serious national anti-corruption programme, recognition was made for the need to secure a strong commitment at the highest political level. However, the following suggestions were made:

- Popular mobilisation against corruption: the most potent force in the fight against corruption is the widespread resentment of corrupt practices and popular support for firm action. Anti-corruption programmes need to be designed to meet the expectations of citizens and with public participation. They are more likely to be effective when they are built on the foundation of popular empowerment, nationally owned and designed to meet national circumstances.

- The private sector and civil society: although an anti-corruption strategy usually focuses initially on preventing the use of public office for private gain, support for greater awareness of the dangers of unethical practices in the private sector and non-governmental institutions would be more widely appreciated. Corrupt behaviour (e.g. by corporate purchasing agents, or in job recruitment) can be as destructive of performance of business or of non-governmental organisations (NGO) as it is of government.

- The need for an international response: there is a strong case on a number of grounds for international co-operation in fighting corruption:

  - countries can learn from each other in the reduction of corruption;

  - in a globalisation economy, transactions across borders are of increasing importance, but are often difficult to monitor by national authorities acting alone;

  - international financial transactions provide opportunities for the laundering of financial gains from corrupt practices.[13]

The Ministers also agreed that, as part of fighting corruption, codes of conduct for politicians, ministers, civil servants and other public officials, should be developed and enforceable. There should be an independent judiciary and legal system capable of enforcing the laws without interference from the practical force. However, an important contribution to the prevention of corruption can be made by strengthening transparency in economic management through:

- full disclosure and examination of government finances, especially by parliamentary scrutiny;
- strengthening of parliamentary public accounts committees;
- the use of open competitive bidding for government contracts;
- publication of full information on the reports of government auditors and evaluations of development projects;
- media access to information on government finances;
- full disclosure of assets by government leaders and their families;
- setting international financial agreements before the legislature and establishing clear guidelines for fiscal discipline;
- establishment of mechanisms for public exposure where the above do not occur.

7. *Leadership, Policy Development and Managing Change*

Support for leadership development and managing change cuts across governance efforts. Effective leadership, essential for a good governance programme, is particularly important when countries are undergoing complex or systematic change involving civil society and private sectors. Effective leadership entails developing the capacities of every one who can increase political and administrative commitment to sustainable human development. Countries need professionals who can translate political vision into a sustained programme for good governance.

The seminars on the Role of the Permanent Secretaries were a clear outcome of good governance as they focused on leadership and change management.

CFTC should seek to support the development of national capacities to articulate goals, policies and strategies, especially those that chart broad national support and consensus. To this end, CFTC could support national institutions that develop the skills of leaders in initiating and managing processes that are systemic and complex and that involve stakeholders and beneficiaries from government, the private sector and civil society. This support would include assistance for training in planning and implementation, building national competence, and developing approaches to public-private partnerships.

8. Civil Service Reform

The reform of state institutions so that they become more efficient, accountable and transparent, is a cornerstone of good governance. Effective reforms require political and administrative will and commitment, which should include the support of the private sector and civil society. Many needs can be addressed, e.g. the formulation of strategies, assessment of capacities, reform of governance rules and procedures, including those for the market and the most vulnerable, review and restructuring of functions and networks; improvement of systems, especially those concerned with planning, management, information and new technologies, budgeting and expenditures, reporting and accountabilities, public-private partnership and decentralisation.

CONCLUSION

The outputs of these governance programmes are many but mention will be made of only a few:

- strengthened cabinet offices which prepare for decision-making and ensure decisions are reflected in departments;

- the establishment of policy units in government which have the capacity and statistical information to assess the impact of expenditure and policies on the poor and the disadvantaged;

- designing transparent mechanisms in government;

- improving performance management systems, e.g. managing the performance of the permanent secretary;

- developing systems which respond to citizens complaints;

- designing appropriate approaches to detection and punishment of corruption at all levels.

In essence, the totality of the Commonwealth Secretariat can be divided into three categories:

(i)   Prevention of corruption through the analysis of the strengths and weaknesses of public policy, with a view to developing strategies to solve potential problems. The civil service reform, for example, can improve the effectiveness of the public service. The tightening of controls over public expenditure and the organisation of workshops on materials management point to the attempt to promote good governance by member states. A code of practice for civil servants has been recommended to a number of countries with a view to reducing and preventing corrupt practice by the civil servants.

(ii)   Strengthening systems and practices that promote good governance and at the same time discourage corruption has been seen as one way in which the Secretariat has made a contribution. The strengthening of public accounts committees, full disclosure and examination of government finances and the use of competitive bidding for government contracts as recommended by member states, at their invitation, constitute a serious attempt to promote good governance.

(iii)   Capacity-building to enhance the capacity of ministries of finance, the public service and the Ombudsman is another kind of assistance given to member states by the Commonwealth Fund for Technical Co-operation. In Ministries of Finance, for example, assistance has been given in order to improve revenue collection and management structures. In the public service, several training programmes have been mounted on human resources development and management, developing strategic plans and redefining the goals and objectives of ministries.

(iv)   At a policy level, Commonwealth Heads of Government at their two-yearly meeting often make declarations in support of a particular initiative or adopt priorities that the Secretariat should put in place. They have made declarations, for example, on promoting public sector reform, human rights and other democratic principles. The principles adopted by Heads of State provide the foundation for concerted action by the Secretariat to promote good governance and combat corruption.

REFERENCES

1.   Government in Transition: A New Paradigm in Public Administration: A report by the Commonwealth Association of Public Administration and Management (CAPAM) on the Conference held in Prince Edward Island, Canada, 28–31 August, 1994.

2.   State of Governance: Mahathir Mohamed, Prime Minister of Malaysia. Public Administration and Development: The International Journal of Management Research and Practice, Vol 18 No. 5, December 1998, p 441.

3.   OECD Ministerial Symposium on the Future of Public Services, held in Paris, March 1996.

4.   Corkery, J. (ed) Governance: evolution of the meaning of the Word in Governance: Concepts and Applications. International Institute of Administrative Sciences, Working group 1999, Brussels, Belgium, p 9.

5.   ibid

6.   Commonwealth Currents, 2/97, p 18.

7.   Unpublished paper: Commonwealth Expert Group on Good Governance and the Elimination of Corruption in Economic Management (1999).

8.   Governance Structures and the Democratic Process: Report of Round Table on Managing Parliamentary – Executive Interface in the

Commonwealth – Cape Town, South Africa, 30 November-4 December 1998, Commonwealth Secretariat.

9. Strengthening Cabinet Decision-making in Commonwealth countries, Commonwealth Secretariat 1999.

10. Agere, S., Redefining Management Roles: Improving the Functional Relationship between Ministers and Permanent Secretaries: Managing the Public Service Strategies for Improvement Series No. 10, Commonwealth Secretariat 1999.

11. World Bank (1989) Strengthening Local Government in Sub-Saharan Africa, EDI Policy Seminar Report No. 21, Washington DC, The World Bank.

12. Smith, B.C. (1993) Choice in the Design of Decentralisation, Commonwealth Secretariat.

13. Report of Commonwealth Finance Ministers and Senior Finance Officials Meetings, Grand Cayman, Cayman Islands (21–23 September, 1999) Commonwealth Secretariat, London.

GOOD GOVERNANCE IN THE PUBLIC SECTOR – PROMOTION AND MANAGEMENT OF PRODUCTIVITY

The concept of good governance is very much inter-linked with institutionalised values such as democracy, observance of human rights and greater efficiency and effectiveness within the public sector. Public management, as a discipline, presents itself with certain techniques, strategies and methods intended to improve the public service reform process and, more importantly, to enable the machinery of government to be cost-conscious and performance-oriented.

Governance, as defined above, is broadly seen as the manner in which power is exercised in the management of a country's economic and social resources for development. From this broad conceptualisation, one is able to derive both the specifics and operational elements that are inherent in good governance. First, it is evident that governance can be divided into three component dimensions: the political, the socio-economic and the dynamic interaction of these two through the process of institutional management.

The main features of good governance can be represented by the following main elements:

(i)   how the people of a country are governed, which is part of the political dimension;

(ii)   how the country's affairs are administered, which is the institutional dimension;

(iii)   the quality of management and institutional capacity to be found in public agencies, and this constitutes the technical dimension.

At the political level, good governance presupposes the implantation of a competitive, multiparty system of democratic politics, respect for human rights and vibrant, unconstrained civil society. Regarding the institutional and technical dimensions, the requirements are a vastly reduced role for the state in economic affairs, a radical programme of public sector reform, credible systems of accountability and transparency with regard to public sector operations and transactions, and an effective judicial framework.[1]

This chapter will focus not on the first dimension but on the second and third, which refer to the institutional and technical dimensions. These two dimensions together constitute the public service or the public administrative system, which is both an instrument of the state as well as the system through which technical competencies are required to implement government policies and programmes.

The emphasis on the institutional and technical dimensions is based on the belief that by getting involved in a narrower and more focused set of tasks, the state is enabled to use more rationally and effectively the limited technical, managerial and professional skills that characterise many of the developing countries, thereby being in a position, it is hoped, to improve the management of residual public sector activities. Derived from this perspective, therefore, is the position that the task of policy reform depends as much on the characteristics of the state itself, the nature of its involvement in economic activity and ordering and, especially, the quality of the central administrative apparatus that is needed to carry out the myriad complex assignments entailed in that process, as on the active involvement of a revitalised private sector.

The rationale for focusing on the administrative machinery is based on the assumption that it is only the strong state that can create a conducive environment in which public sector reform can be meaningfully and effectively managed. The state remains central to the process of structural change and to the delivery of service to the public. The state is responsible for identifying institutional deficiencies and for driving the public service reform process, thereby strengthening the technical capabilities of the state. In strengthening the public service, it is assumed that productivity will improve and that its capacity to deliver the service will be a noticeable result. Some of the objectives of the reform efforts have been:

(i)   the rationalisation, in terms of its size and functions, of the overall public sector;
(ii)   the introduction of more effective systems of financial accountability;
(ii)   greater transparency in the operations of public institutions;
(iv)   the upgrading of the skills base of the sector and the modernisation of its functional principles, procedures and systems; and
(v)   the development of a realistic remuneration policy.

The issues of productivity addressed in this section are a means of implementing these reforms. After all, one of the reasons for introducing administrative reform was because productivity and performance had declined tremendously. The reforms were therefore conceptualised as a contributory factor towards increased productivity and better performance by the public servants in the delivery of service. The emphasis in this section is, therefore, to strengthen the institution and instrument of the state and to build a capacity to deliver efficiently public goods and services. The details of strengthening institutional capacity are discussed as an attempt to sustain good governance, which would be impossible to achieve without an effective instrument. An effective administrative machinery must therefore be productive and provide high-impact, low-cost services. Institutional capacity strengthening includes amongst other issues, human resources, financial management, organisational structure and management systems, and policy-making processes.

MANAGING PRODUCTIVITY

This section discusses the role of public administration in the promotion and management of productivity and performance in the pursuit of economic growth and sustainable development. Public administration is conceptualised as an instrument or machinery of the state. Like all instruments of state, public administration is generally and deliberately designed in a manner that it is capable of achieving the stated goals, which in this case, are economic growth, sustainable development, and efficient delivery of service to the public.

The nature and type of productivity will be discussed in relation to the social, political and economic environment within which it operates and to which it should be responsive and finally accountable. Public institutions, as used here, refer to civil or public service, local authorities and public enterprises or parastatals, which together constitute the public sector. However, emphasis will be placed on the public or civil service, which is a lead institution within the public sector in that it initiates rules and regulations governing the establishment and management of public enterprises. Within the context of public service, productivity is defined as the efficient utilisation of resources, e.g. labour, capital, land, time, materials, energy and information, in the production of various goods and services. Increased or higher productivity would imply the accomplishment of more with the same amount of resources or achieving higher output in terms of quantity and quality for the same input. It is in this context that society expects public administration as a machinery of government to produce the desired results of achieving economic growth and sustainable development in an efficient manner.

Performance management, as used in this context, is the use of performance measurement in shaping the performance of the public service and public servants alike. Performance, therefore, refers to the process or instrumentality of increasing or improving productivity, given adequate resources.

RATIONALE

Although productivity is becoming a fashionable concept in the delivery of public service and in the promotion of good governance, it emanates from various sources of different interests. In general, there are at least five different sources:

1. The consumers of public services are by far the largest group that demands the efficient delivery of services. Both the business community and civil society require and sometimes demand that the services delivered to them by public servants be efficient and effective. The customs officer, for example, would be expected to process the application of an investor or goods earmarked for investment in order to promote economic growth and development policy. The consumers of such development policy are not only the business community but also the people who are likely to benefit when employment is generated as a result of appropriate investment. In many third world countries it is quite common to find that the government formulates a policy on accelerating investment but the public servant who is supposed to implement that policy has not been sensitised or behaves in direct contradiction to the spirit and intent of the policy. If a customs officer is corrupt, or demands certain favours before the goods are cleared, then that officer is an impediment to the promotion of an investment policy and consequently discourages the would-be investor.

    Such kind of behaviour exhibited by the public servant is inefficient, ineffective and negatively affects productivity and negates good governance promotion. This behaviour pattern shown by the civil servant is certainly common in many ministries responsible for the delivery of services to consumers. In rural communities for example, villagers demand the improvement of their quality of life through the provision of clean water supply, sanitation, the construction of health centres and roads. The pressures for better services are imposed on representatives of people in civil society. Civil society is important because it holds the state to account for its performance. The mass media, voluntary organisations, professional and consumer organisations demand that services are delivered efficiently.

2. Politicians or the representatives of civil society also demand that services delivered to their constituencies are meaningful and offered at the appropriate time. In countries where there are different political parties, the competition amongst the politicians to provide better services is even greater. The basis of such a competition is not only for humanitarian purposes but also for self-interest on the part of the politician so that he or she can be elected again to represent his/her people. Some politicians are known to be very critical of the public servants in the delivery of services. Ministers complain that the policies that have been formulated by Cabinet are sometimes ignored or are executed half-heartedly. In other countries for example, ministers have accused the Ministry of Lands for not accelerating the allocation of land to the peasants. Ministries of Health and Education have not escaped the blame on poor education and indiscipline among teachers and, equally, the deteriorating health services where the shortage or absence of drugs is the order of the day. In some developed countries, politicians have complained about the increasing hospital waiting lists. The blame has been placed on those who deliver the health services. When the services are not efficiently provided, a conflict arises between the legislature and bureaucracy, or put differently, between the politician and the civil servant who is employed by the state. The conflicts and competition between and among the various interest groups brings pressure to bear on public servants to perform better and, above all, to achieve the set goals. In some instances conflicts of this nature arise out of lack of clarity of organisational goals or out of inconsistencies in policy formulation and implementation, both by the bureaucracy and state.

3. The private sector, where it exists, has demanded that better services be provided so that it can generate economic growth, which may result in the creation of employment, a goal required and appreciated by the government.

The reorganisation of the economy taking place in most countries entails, amongst other measures, the promotion and development of the private sector. Private enterprise as a philosophy and policy is understood and accepted by many governments as an engine of development. If this assumption is correct, then the engine must be well looked after and must be facilitated to provide its services and perform its functions efficiently.

The Chambers of Commerce and Industry, representatives of industrial and financial capital, labour and landowners generally have dialogue with governments so that a climate conducive to increased productivity is created. Such dialogue has brought the scrutiny of public servants to the fore in their attempt to deliver services to the stakeholders of the economy. The management principles and practices in the conduct of business in the private sector have been assumed to lead to efficiency and effectiveness. Many governments are under pressure to practise management tools that have been found to be effective in the private sector. The setting up of performance targets, performance measurements, pay-related performance, performance contracts, mission statements etc. are all attempts to improve productivity in the private sector. These attempts, where they have been useful, are now being implemented by many governments during the reform programme of the economy and bureaucracy.

4. Public servants who on one hand constitute the delivery of service system can on the other hand also be the recipients of service. They, as members of civil society, as parents and as farmers are also recipients of service in their various statuses in society. They therefore also experience the effects of a poor administrative system. As citizens they also apply for passports, for example, and whatever inefficiency is exhibited by the passport office, they also experience it. In their different capacities they also complain about inefficiency in the civil service. In addition, they are also voters responsible for the election of representatives of parliament, councils and other formal organisations. In this regard they are consumers while at the same time they are part of the system that delivers the service to the public.

However, even as civil servants, or providers of services, they can complain about the inadequate inputs from the government. In some cases there has been a lot of under-funding, under-manning and under-provision of certain facilities, which would enable civil servants to provide services efficiently. If there are not enough nurses and drugs, teachers and classrooms etc. the services rendered by the health and teaching professions will be negatively affected.

5. Donor community and non-governmental organisations often demand that their aid be used effectively. Such demands are expressed amid allegations that aid is not trickling down to the right people at the right time. In other words, aid is not reaching the target groups. In such circumstances, aid is not productive to the extent that it does not produce the desired results.

In order to ensure that aid becomes productive, some donors have sought ways of avoiding bureaucracy and instead have set up community groups who have direct access to the donors. Some other donors always carry out impact assessment surveys, which will indicate whether the aid was put to good use or not. In some instances, governments have come under pressure from non-governmental organisations on the rules and regulations that impede the successful transfer of resources to the target groups. International organisations also demand that their assistance be used effectively. Productivity therefore becomes a critical factor in the management of donor assistance programmes. Efficiency and effectiveness are all matters of great concern to both the providers and the recipients of assistance. As a result of these pressures on the government, many public institutions are being reformed in order to suit the new demands. The policy of decentralisation is an attempt to ensure that the resources are administered by a system that is close to the consumers of services. It is equally true that the hiving off of certain functions from the public sector to the private sector is an admission by a highly centralised bureaucracy. The organisation of a bureaucracy, which leads to the transfer of power to the local groups or institutions, also serves as a political instrument of demonstrating the responsiveness to the needs of the community.

TYPOLOGY OF PRODUCTIVITY

In analysing the nature and type of productivity, it is possible to identify the form and manner in which it takes shape at a conceptual and practical level. Conceptually, some types of productivity are ideology-oriented while others are purely based on the needs and demands of both the providers and recipients of services. Ideological underpinnings are reflected in the programmes that for example emphasise the principles of a market economy while others are dictated by the principles of equity, equal opportunities and access to services. The following are the various types of productivity as reflected in the implementation process:

- Many of the reforms are quantitative in nature and are driven purely by the fact of numbers. Many public services in the developing countries, for example, have been under pressure to reduce the numbers of civil servants on the payroll and the costs of maintaining such a large bureaucracy. The large numbers of public employees are not only observed in the public service but also in the public enterprises or parastatals, local authorities and statutory organisations. As a result of these large numbers many governments have used the cutback approach, which has been known by various names such as downsizing, de-layering, rationalisation or right-sizing.

- The downsizing of the service has, in some instances, been arbitrary in that no studies were conducted which indicated that the service was too big by a certain percentage. Many countries were advised to cut down by twenty-five per cent without showing how the figure was calculated. The same figure has been applied in different countries with different sizes of population and needs. The cutback approach has been applied even in circumstances where the need does not arise or does not address a problem. In 1991, the UNDP facilitated a study of about ten African countries on the size and cost of the civil service. The studies showed that the reduction in the size and cost of the civil service alone did not result automatically in efficiency and effectiveness.[2] Further, there was no rationale for the reduction by the same 25 per cent in many countries. Similar studies conducted in the South Pacific Island states, the Caribbean and Asian countries have revealed the experiences of cut-back management approach by the similar percentage. The assumption that productivity can be enhanced under conditions of reduced numbers alone has not correlated with improved efficiency. However, there are incidences in which the economy cannot support the large size of the public service, especially where there were large numbers of non-existent (ghosts) posts.

- Many reforms of the public services have been qualitative in nature. They have been driven by the demands for better quality of service delivered to consumers. The poor quality of service has, in some cases, been associated with the poor quality of civil servants recruited, poor remuneration of civil servants, corruption and lack of commitment to work. Low morale has also contributed to the lowering of standards and poor quality of service. The quality of service has been one of the most significant factors in the reform of public sector institutions. The changes driven by quality have resulted in the redesigning of organisational structure, redefinition of and setting of institutional goals, changes in management styles, approaches and skills, improved rewards, recognition of service, improved morale of civil servants and the designing of performance appraisal systems.

One of the major criticisms of public enterprises has been associated with the increased salaries of Chief Executives without a corresponding increase in the quality of service. The same argument is also now posed for those public enterprises which were privatised whose Chief Executives earn enormous amounts of money with little evidence of improvement in the delivery of service. In some cases, the costs of providing the same service have increased. In the United Kingdom there is a big debate on the performance of the newly privatised utilities such as Telecommunications, Electricity, Water,

Railways. In the railways, the fares have gone up without a corresponding increase in improved service. For example, some trains do not come on time, causing delays at work places.

- The majority of reforms are finance-driven. They arise out of the need to save money or to reduce public expenditure with the hope that productivity will improve. Most reforms on reduction on public expenditure have been made conditionalities for aid by some international organisations. Within governments, negotiations have been conducted between Ministries of Finance and financial institutions. In some countries, such decisions are never debated in government ministries but instructions are given to public institutions without studies having been conducted and decisions made based on accurate information.

  Public enterprises have been targets, especially in the reduction of subsidies by the state. Some of the public enterprises have argued that while it may be necessary to reduce subsidies, studies should be conducted to indicate where and when they can be reduced and be made clear.

  From mere observation, the reduction in subsidies to the public enterprise does not always lead to increased productivity or better performance. There are other variables that have to be taken into account. One of the biggest problems experienced by some governments is that the decision to cut down subsidies is arrived at secretly between one ministry and international institutions. The stakeholders themselves are always left out when such negotiations take place. This is a point we may need to take into account during future aid negotiations with international and multilateral agencies.

- The fourth type of productivity is related to the mere reduction of human resources in public enterprises. The assumption given is that the reduction of numbers of personnel will result in savings. While this may be true, it does not directly result in efficiency or more productivity. In some countries, certain favourable packages have been prepared for those who are leaving the public enterprise or those who have been made redundant. In other countries, it is the efficient and hard working people who have taken advantage of such packages leaving behind the dead wood. Some of those made redundant have been successful in their newly found enterprises while other professionals contract with government as consultants and are paid more than what they were earning when they were employees of government or public enterprises.

In such situations the salary bill of the public enterprises is not therefore reduced although the numbers of employees has statistically been curtailed.

The dead wood that remains in government cannot be expected to increase efficiency because they were never productive in the first place. Under these circumstances, efficiency has not been achieved even if the numbers of employees has been reduced. These examples should make governments aware that acceptance of recommendations without conducting further studies will lead to the contradictions and conflicts explained above. It should be made clear that productivity cannot be achieved by the mere factor of reduction of numbers alone.

- There are at least two sources from which reforms emanate. First, there is a type of productivity recommended by external sources, which is related to monetary policies. International institutions submit recommendations which are financial in nature and which aim to solve a financial problem in accordance with their mandate. There are also some internally determined methods of improving efficiency of the service. In general, such methods involve many organs of government, they are owned by the government and can be modified by the same if it is found necessary. The internally driven constitute a process approach in which there is the widest possible consultation between and among stakeholders.

It would appear that many governments opt for externally determined approaches to increased productivity because they are desperate to secure loans and credit facilities with international institutions. Then, in desperation, they accept the conditionalities without careful study with the hope that they will resolve the problem. Experience from the results of many studies should be lessons for many of us who have not yet started such kind of reforms. All that is being advocated here is that the leaders of the reform programme should conduct studies to determine the kind of recommendations which they should take before they are implemented.

PROMOTION OF PRODUCTIVITY

Experience has shown that it is necessary to build in conditions that can promote and accelerate efficiency within ministries or public enterprises. Such conditions should be put in place from day one of forming an organisation or designing a ministry. The conditions should be closely monitored, evaluated and reformed when necessary rather than wait until the situation has deteriorated to a level not redeemable. Some of the critical factors that can accelerate efficiency and effectiveness and overall performance of the public sector are discussed below.

The recruitment of qualified, experienced and competent staff should be seriously addressed at the time that they are being selected. There are now modern techniques that are used to minimise the selection of incompetent people. The interviews, examinations or taking up of references should be followed. In order to recruit the right people it is necessary to make the job description, job evaluation and objectives of the organisation very clear. In general, it is good to form a committee that is responsible for the recruitment of staff rather than rely on the one head of department. The committees help to reduce the allegations of corruption or nepotism. In addition, the committee should be so selected as to minimise gender, race and ethnic bias. The right people should be recruited for the right jobs.

- Once staff have been recruited, induction courses should be organised for them to appreciate the kind of an organisation in which they are working. The old staff should also be sent continuously for staff development courses and exposed to internally designed training programmes. Many ministries do not have a training vote; if they have, there is very little money allocated for that purpose. Training is often appreciated by government, although it is generally under-funded, under-manned and equipped with inadequate material resources. Induction courses can also be organised for new members of parliament in order to increase their performance. In the UK, the study, Rethinking Representation, suggested a more thorough and non-partisan induction for new MPs, including information on parliamentary processes and an informal code of conduct for constituency work.

The result of poor funding by governments on training is that the donor community prepares and makes available programmes for the region in order to minimise costs. The programmes may not be suitable and geared to a specific country and it is generic in nature. If it is a regional course then there are very few people who can afford to attend. As a result, the training becomes inadequate for the entire staff. However, sometimes training programmes are available but the problem has been in selecting the staff who should undergo training. Favouritism has crept into the selection process, resulting in the wrong people attending courses. Those who really need training are often left behind and poor performance at work continues and services are not delivered efficiently.

There are also attitudinal problems regarding training. First the local training programmes or programmes prepared by local training institutions are often looked down on and despised. Secondly, the short courses offered abroad are often over-subscribed, even for low-level managers. In some countries, it has been observed that senior managers go for overseas courses, even if the courses are meant for low and middle-level managers. Investment in human resources is not, therefore, appropriately allocated.

- The third area requiring attention at the outset is the proper designing of administrative and management structures so that the public enterprise can achieve its goals. Sometimes, organisational structures that are recommended do not suit particular goals. Structures must be dynamic and must suit the needs of the organisation. Most governments prefer hierarchically organised structures, even in situations where flat structures are appropriate. The design of the structure, and the goals of the enterprise should be the key factors in the selection process of personnel. Highly centralised structures tend to delay communication within the organisation, resulting in inefficiency. The structures should be so designed as to minimise the areas for duplication of functions, which may also lead to inefficiency and ineffectiveness of the enterprise. The appropriately designed management structure has a potential of forecasting possible capacity to deliver goods and services efficiently.

- Target-setting and clarity of the organisation's objectives are some of the ways in which efficiency and effectiveness can be ensured. It is possible to measure the productivity of an individual in an organisation. In many ministries, permanent secretaries have been unable to measure the performance of an officer mainly because the objectives were not clearly defined and there were no specific measurable tasks assigned by management. The review of organisational goals which has been necessitated by the Economic Structural Adjustment programmes has shown, in many countries, that some very senior officials were ignorant about the goals of their ministry or public enterprise. If they were ignorant about their goals and at the same time expected to be productive, it is inconceivable that they would be in a position to measure their efficiency as well as the effectiveness of their colleagues and their subordinates. Some officials in government have argued that it is not possible to formulate measurement criteria for service ministries such as Education, Health, the Police and Information Services. This is a mere rationalisation of the argument, as it is now known that it is possible to draw up criteria for the measurement of service ministries.

- It is now recognised, following various studies on public administration, that a socially good environment within which the public service operates and the promotion of high morale of public servants contribute to increased efficiency of the civil service. Increased morale of civil servants is determined by a number of factors within the political and economic environment. The improvement in the conditions of service, including salary adjustments, all play a part in ensuring that civil servants maintain their high morale with consequential effects on their efficiency. The civil service can easily become corrupt if the conditions of service deteriorate and there are no opportunities for improvement. Corrupt practices do not contribute to good productivity of the service. The Heads of the Civil Service would need to be aware of the impact of these factors, which enable their public services to perform better. The reform of the public service taking place in many countries must take these factors into account. At the beginning of the reform process, there is often emphasis on the strategy, structure, systems and skills to the exclusion of staff and their conditions of service. The conditions are often thought of well after the systems have been changed. In such cases, conflicts have arisen with the civil servants following the reform process. These conflicts also result in the low morale of public servants who may be uncertain about their future, career path and job security.

THE MANAGEMENT OF PRODUCTIVITY

In the recent past, it was often recognised that increased productivity was the result of a combination of factors such as labour, materials and supervision. It was assumed that the presence of a manager alone to supervise employees would result in increased productivity. Within the public service, it was assumed that if a ministry had a permanent secretary or a director then the rules and regulations would be applied to the subordinates. The rules would be strengthened by threats of firm disciplinary measures, some of which included suspension, dismissal or reduction of remuneration. While these factors could be effective, modern management practices indicate that the public service could be more productive if it moved away from the rigid and punitive role to a catalytic or facultative role. In this regard, the public service is expected to apply some of the management practices that have, all along, been the domain of the private sector.

Permanent secretaries, for example, would now be expected to behave like businessmen in the management of the ministries or public enterprises. They are expected to take decisions, consider cost-effective measures and take into account the needs and aspirations of the consumers and society at large. The services, therefore, must suit consumers, not consumers suit bureaucracy.

These new approaches to the management of public bureaucracy also affect the way in which the Heads of the Civil Service relate to their colleagues and the entire management of the public service. The business approach assumes that at the end of the inputs there must be a product which is cost-effective and which is appreciated by the customer. The acquisition of a business approach depends upon the attitude of the manager, management skills and commitment to make an improvement in the delivery of service. Quite often, there can develop a contradiction between the approach and the rules. This is particularly noticeable in situations where attitudes change and skills improve but the rules and regulations remain static. In many Commonwealth countries, the permanent secretary is the accounting officer of the ministry and is accountable to parliament through the Public Accounts Committee. As an accounting officer, he might be scared to delegate for fear that he will be called to answer questions from the Public Accounts Committee. In such circumstances, he would be reluctant to delegate unless the rules of the game were altered to suit the new approaches.

During the reform process of the civil service, the Heads of the Civil Service play a critically important role in ensuring that efficiency is maintained and that redefined goals and tasks are achieved. A few of the ways in which Heads of Civil Service might manage and sustain efficiency of the civil service are suggested below:

- The management of interface between the minister and the permanent secretary is crucial in the reform process. The minister and the permanent secretary are the leaders of the reform of the ministry in which the minister represents the political will and society while the permanent secretary represents the civil service machinery. The two need to work together and to be committed to change or reform. If one of them does not appreciate or support the reform, there will be undermining of positions by each other. If there is a conflict between them, it is bound to affect the civil service machinery and the reform process may be derailed. If such a situation arises, the Head of the Civil Service has to be aware of it and should take appropriate measures to ensure that efficiency is maintained and that the reform process not derailed. If need be, the Head of State and government should be advised of the existence of such a relationship in a ministry.

The sustenance of productivity would require back-up administrative support and political commitment from the top. This is necessary because the reform process has inherent contradictions that must be grasped by the Head of the Civil Service. In some cases, ministers have been known to be openly critical of permanent secretaries and civil servants during the reform of the service. Such criticisms do not give credibility to the system, particularly if they come from the civil society. Genuine criticisms are welcome and it may be a question of how they are handled and at what point in time. The civil service is an instrument of the state and should therefore be seen to be supported by the state and if there are grounds for change then the reforms should be put into effect.

In some governments, reforms have been implemented in some ministries and not in others. The lack of uniform implementation of reform is likely to create inconsistencies within the reform process of the entire civil service that may result in different regulations for different ministries. One of the causes for such inconsistencies is that the minister and the permanent secretary in one ministry may be opposed to reform based on different self-interests.

It should be pointed out that the relationship between the minister and permanent secretary is by far the most difficult to manage because the two represent different and sometimes even conflicting interests, constituencies and mandates:

- The co-operation, co-ordination and collaboration of all stakeholders in the civil service reform should be cultivated and sustained by the Head of the Civil Service. The co-operation should not only be seen to operate under the civil service but also between public and private sector, including civil society. In order to facilitate such collaboration, information must be made available and, where possible, research findings published to be followed by public debates. The main reason for involving the private sector and other civic organisations is that public service reforms have an impact on the latter. If, for example, certain functions of the civil service are to be hived off to the private sector then it is important that the sector be aware of what it is that it is to absorb and with what skills and resources. In some cases, there can be an interchangeability of skills and resources and this is only possible if there is co-operation. Because of the historical past there has been animosity, hatred and suspicions between the two sectors.

In the reform process, there are at least three lead ministries and these are the President's Office, or Head of State, the Ministry of Finance and the Ministry of Public Service responsible for personnel and administration. Finance and Human Resource Ministries should co-operate and consult with each other under the leadership of the Head of the Civil Service. In some countries, Ministries of Finance have made decisions, for example, to cut down the number of civil servants in order to reduce the budget deficit without consulting the ministry responsible for human resources.

■ The accessibility of the Head of Civil Service to permanent secretaries is important in ensuring that no barriers are erected in the consultation process. In some countries there exists fear or mistrust between the Head of the Civil Service and permanent secretaries. The openness, personality and interest of the Head of the Civil Service reduce these obstacles to close collaboration and consultations. The accessibility of the Head of the Civil Service should be accompanied by tolerance, understanding and an appreciation of the problems experienced by individual permanent secretaries. In discussing the role of management in promoting productivity, Simuyemba, an expert on productivity states that, "Management looks at the resources at its exposure, obtains facts about each one of them, individually and collectively plans, directs, co-ordinates, controls and motivates in order to produce goods and services. Managers play a central and vital role in co-ordinating resources.[3]

The Head of the Civil Service plays these central co-ordinating roles that in some respects may appear contradictory in that some managers would find it difficult to make a distinction between control and motivating efforts practised by one manager at any given time.

Within the public service, the Head of the Civil Service could accelerate productivity among civil servants through:

- appropriate changes in managerial styles and practices;
- devising suitable management development and training;
- programmes – managers learn every day;
- introduction of productivity incentive schemes;
- strengthening of management training institutions and not fighting them or becoming jealous of them, or ignoring them;
- offering awards where efficiency is outstanding and to say thank you for a job well done.

■ Productivity could be made a conditionality for budget allocation. In many countries, budgets are determined by the needs of the ministry and in particular by the previous year's allocation. "Productivity measures are rarely used to justify budget and staff requirements. The present budget is taken as a base and increases are added to meet increasing service demands, ignoring that the latter could be provided through productivity improvement without additional resources. Thus, the size of the budget and the large numbers of staff in the ministry tend to be regarded as a status symbol." [4]

In some cases, the salaries of Chief Executives are determined by the huge budgets and the number of employees in the public enterprise. They are therefore a source of power, authority and influence. These views and benchmarks should be reviewed in order to ensure that efficiency and effectiveness are achieved and maintained.

BARRIERS TO PRODUCTIVITY

Productivity is often hindered by the following factors:

- under-funding of a ministry or a public enterprise;
- under-manning and overstaffing departments;
- misallocation of human and financial resources;
- absence of financial discipline;
- absence of regular monitoring of performance;
- corrupt practices, nepotism and favouritism;
- absence of code of conduct and guidelines;
- absence of set targets and performance appraisals etc.;
- poor leadership;
- low morale of employees;
- lack of ownership and involvement in the design of performance agreements, goals and functions.

When all the factors that improve productivity have been strengthened and all the barriers to increased performance have been minimised, mechanisms should be worked out which would ensure that public servants are accountable for their behaviour and their performance in the work place. As discussed earlier, good governance can be strengthened by the extent to which the public servants are held accountable for their public duties and responsibilities.

REFERENCES

1. Ferguson, T. (1995) Structural Adjustment and Good Governance: The Case for Guyana Public Affairs Consulting Enterprise, p 161.

2. United Nations: Study on Size and Cost of Civil Service in Africa: 1991, New York.

3. Simuyemba, Planning for a Measuring Productivity in the Public Service in African Management Development Forum, Vol 2. No. 1, March 1991.

4. Commonwealth Secretariat: From Problem to Solution, Commonwealth Strategies for Reform. Managing the Public Service Strategies for Improvement Series, No. 1.

ACCOUNTABILITY AND TRANSPARENCY
IN THE PUBLIC SERVICE

This chapter focuses on two critical dimensions of accountability: political administrative and financial accountability, with reference to the linkages to administrative efficiency and economic performance. It reviews the main methods of enforcing accountability and includes illustrations from both developed and developing countries. In highlighting recent trends in this area, attention is drawn to the impact of the on-going democratisation process in public accountability and some examples of good and bad practices are cited. Finally, the implications of increased attention to accountable governance for training are examined, with suggestions on specialised training programmes for politicians, judicial officials, accountants and auditors and journalists.

INTRODUCTION

Accountability and Transparency in Public Sector

The importance of accountability as an aspect of good governance is derived from the definition discussed in chapter one. The UNDP has defined good governance as the exercise of political, economic and administrative authority in the management of a country's affairs at all levels. Good governance, according to the definition, has a number of attributes. It is effective, participatory, transparent, accountable, productive, and equitable and promotes the rule of law. However, the major attribute is the exercise of power and authority over the country's affairs. The exercise of power, while shared by many agencies of government, should have checks and balances so that no one part of the machinery has absolute power. One of the ways in which these checks and balances work is to make the systems, structures, organisation and staff become accountable for their responsibilities, functions, tasks and behaviour in the work place.

In a number of third world countries, the central concern of good governance in relation to the exercise of power and the operation of public sectors, is the pervasive corruption that has tended to characterise them. It was evident in some countries that a culture of corruption had become embedded in the public bureaucracy in environments of extreme scarcities and depressed emoluments. In such a context, the absence of accountability compounded matters and came to be a defining feature of the administrative culture over a certain period.

41

The basic instruments of accountability include legislative reviews of a ministry's activities, periodic audit reports on public expenditure, and the practice of questioning ministers in parliament on on-going activities. Political leaders and legislatures act as surrogates for the public in the system of democratic accountability. These public accountability mechanisms have fallen into disuse over the years. For example, at the end of the 1980s the preparation and presentation for parliamentary scrutiny of public accounts statements were behind schedule by almost a decade. This was particularly evident in some one-party states, and it was silent or absent in military dictatorships and regimes. Some one-party states regarded the pursuit of public accountability as unpatriotic or causing embarrassment to the ruling party. The reason why some regimes would behave in such a manner is that the exercise of political and economic power was challenged through the instruments of government such as the Comptroller and Auditor-General who was hated by some officials. A lesson that can be drawn from these experiences is that countries must never allow themselves to degenerate into a situation where corruption becomes the culture of the officials holding public office. Once corruption becomes embedded in a culture it is extremely difficult to remove its elements from the political and administrative system. It is the greatest threat to the success of public policy, to the achievement of sustainable human development and to the successful management of economic and social resources.

One of the main issues in the evolving democratisation process in many countries is the extent to which public officials are held accountable for their actions. The most visible yardstick is the phenomenon of competitive elections that allow citizens to give mandates to those who seek to exercise political power. Other methods of enforcing the accountability of the "governors" (both elected and appointed) to the "governed" include parliamentary institutions, judicial institutions and specialised institutions like the Ombudsman. Enforcement of accountability can also be enhanced through decentralised structures of government, through mechanisms for public participation in the conduct of government business, and through the oversight role of the mass media and public opinion. There are also internal control measures within governmental bureaucracies, usually involving checks on the conduct of the permanent appointed officials, enforced directly by the temporary, elected officials and through rules and regulations associated with the systems for managing the core personnel and finance functions. For obvious reasons, the combination of methods would vary from one country to another, depending on the historical, social, economic and political realities in each country.

The first part of this chapter is devoted to a brief discussion of the three dimensions of accountability – political, administrative and financial accountability – with references to the linkages to administrative efficiency and economic performance. This is followed by a review of the methods of enforcing accountability, with examples drawn from both developed and developing countries. The third section reviews recent trends in Sub-Saharan Africa with particular attention to some examples of good and bad practices. The concluding section highlights the implications of increased attention on accountability for training.

TWO DIMENSIONS OF ACCOUNTABILITY

Two dimensions of accountability are commonly distinguished in the literature: political and financial accountability. *Political accountability* is generally associated with electoral mandate, which refers to the mandate that citizens give to politicians who constitute the executive and legislative arms of government. Normally, the tenure of both the political executive and the legislature is temporary because electoral mandate is subject to the outcome of elections that are held at periodic intervals. In countries where electoral mandates are genuine (elections are free and fair and the results are respected), citizens use the power of their votes to keep in power those politicians that have performed satisfactorily – who "delivered the goods" – and to reject the poor performers – "throwing out the rascals". Genuine electoral mandates confer legitimacy on governments and help to guarantee their credibility, as well as the stability and predictability of their policies. The alternatives to electoral legitimacy are various forms of authoritarianism such as the governmental systems of the former soviet bloc, one-party systems and military governments. In the case of military governments, there is a reliance on the "legitimacy of the gun"; the military leaders who govern derive their power from the "barrel of a gun". By definition, authoritarian governments lack accountability, and this affects the quality of governance. The alternative of an unaccountable but visionary, authoritarian political leadership committed to a developmental ideology and the production of quality services to the public, as witnessed is some South-East Asian countries, is an exception.[1]

---

[1] The following is an instructive interpretation of the South-East Asian experience: "to have in power authoritarians whose monomaniacal aim is to make their countries' economies grow – meaning to serve the whole nation's interest. Authoritarians without this aim are worse than elected politicians. With it they have consistently proved the better rulers in poor Asia." See "The dilemma of

Financial accountability focuses sharply on the breed for accurate and timely reporting on the utilisation of funds, usually through professionally audited accounts. In the public sector, the objective is to ensure that public funds have been used for the purposes for which they were approved and that they have been used economically and efficiently. The key issues here are the timeliness in the preparation of accounts and their auditing, the quality of auditing, especially the attention paid to performance and value for money, and the enforcement of sanctions in case of fraud, mismanagement or theft. In situations where external financial assistance is involved, either through borrowing from multilateral financial institutions or through development assistance provided by donors, the accounting and auditing standards of the institutions and governments concerned have to be respected. This is the explanation for the strong emphasis on international accounting and auditing standards in the discussion of financial accountability. The results of good financial accountability are used for making decisions on resource mobilisation and allocation, and to assess the efficiency with which resources are used. They can also be used by the public and stakeholders (for example, donors) to assess the performance of governments against agreed objectives.[2]

Administrative Accountability refers to the obligation to answer for the fulfilment of assigned and accepted duties within the framework of the authority and resources provided. Defined in this manner, administrative accountability generally applies to public servants, particularly permanent secretaries, directors, heads of department or chief executives of public enterprises. These sets of public officials are not elected but appointed on technical competencies. The officials are generally allocated a budget by parliament and are expected to produce the results with the resources allocated to them.

In general, accountability has come into loose usage. It is common to speak of the accountability that public servants owe to their political and administrative superiors. Polidano (1998) makes a distinction between direct and indirect

---

democracy," *The Economist* (London), October 30, 1993. Some people would add Pinochet's Chile to this category of countries. In SSA, this combination of authoritarianism and a development orientation was unknown during the decades of authoritarian rule in the region.

[2]   Some of the points in this paragraph are drawn from J. Makanda, "Financial accountability and economic performance in sub-Saharan Africa," Capacity Building and Implementation Division, Africa Technical Department the World Bank, Washington, Washington, D.C., September 1994, processed.

accountability. Indirect accountability refers to being accountable to outsiders such as the public, consumers or client groups, whereas direct accountability amounts to accountability upwards through the chain of command. Polidano identifies three main elements of accountability:

- Power of Prior Approval that refers the authority to regulate the behaviour of bureaucrats by subjecting them to procedural requirements and making them obtain clearance before taking certain decisions. This mode of accountability is traditionally associated with central agencies of government (though departments may also set rules or standards of their own).

  Power of prior approval is a form of internal control within a particular ministry and is used to set procedural safeguards on staffing, expenditure and other administrative functions. In essence, the safeguards inform the top officials what to do and what not to do. In the Westminster model of government, such rules are generally referred to as Treasury Instructions. The authority to spend, for example, has to be obtained from Treasury even if the item is budgeted for within that financial year.

- Role accountability refers to an official's answerability for fulfilling his or her core role – the duties which he or she was hired to carry out in the first place. It is essentially accountability for results: this is at the forefront of the new public management movement. It may rely on formal performance targets as related to the new public management.

- Retrospective review refers to the after-event scrutiny of a department's operations by bodies external to the department, such as audit offices, parliamentary committees, ombudsmen, and the courts. In this category, one may also include bodies outside the state, such as the press and pressure groups. The element of subjectivity and unpredictability in the review can vary depending on its nature and the body undertaking it.

The significance of accountability in public service lies in the strong linkages between it and the goals of administrative efficiency and good economic performance. In many cases, weakness in accountability is an important explanatory factor for such shortcomings in public management as poor service delivery, inability to mobilise resources, waste or mismanagement of available resources and neglect of the maintenance of public goods and equipment. With regard to economic performance, economic policies formulated by governments that are accountable tend to enjoy greater credibility and stability

45

than is the case with governments that are not accountable. Credibility and stability of economic policies directly affect the level of both local and foreign investment. Further illustrations of these linkages and their consequences are highlighted in the following two sections on the methods of enforcing accountability and recent trends in sub-Saharan Africa.

METHODS OF ENFORCING ACCOUNTABILITY

As mentioned in the introduction, accountability can be enforced through elections, parliamentary legislative control, judicial control, ombudsmen, decentralised structures of government, public participation, the mass media and internal administrative control measures. The role of elections in enforcing accountability was highlighted in the discussion of political accountability. In most modern states, the constitution contains provisions on the relationships among the three arms of government: the executive, the legislature and the judiciary. Normally, the provisions include requirements for the legislature to control the executive and for the judiciary to control both the executive and the legislature. Since the executive arm of government refers to both the political executive and the permanent career officials who are jointly responsible for the conduct of government business, legislative and judicial controls extend to the two groups of officials.

Legislative control: In many countries, the legislature maintains oversight of the conduct of government business through debates and the work of a varying number of committees. Where legislative committees are effective, they help enhance the quality of policy-making (increasing their responsiveness to citizens' needs and demands), check abuses of government power through their investigations, and monitor performance. One good example in parliamentary systems of government is the role of a Public Accounts Committee (PAC) which undertakes *a posteriori* control of government expenditures. Its work is based on the annual reports of the Auditor General who is normally independent of the executive. This represents a critical meeting point of political and financial accountability. Where PACs are effective, they help to enhance efficiency as well as check financial mismanagement.

In Britain, the established practice is that a prominent leader of the opposition party in parliament chairs the PAC and senior civil servants who are responsible for financial management in ministries and departments (they, are referred to in this role as accounting officers), are personally summoned before the PAC to answer any queries and adverse comments made in the Auditor

General's report. It is important to stress that effective use of PACs depends on the capacity of the Auditor General's Office, the ability of the PAC members and the publicity that is given to both the hearings and the sanctions that are imposed (if any). It is the absence of a combination of two or more of these factors that explains the ineffectiveness of PACs in some SSA countries that have established British-style parliamentary system of government (for example, Kenya, Nigeria and Tanzania).

Another illustration of legislative control is the work of investigative or select committees such as the famous US Congressional Committee that probed the Watergate scandal. (Another congressional committee is currently probing the Whitewater scandal). The British parliamentary tradition of "Question Time", which has been adapted in several other countries (e.g. France) also provides an opportunity for legislators to expose cases of incompetence and maladministration recorded by the executive on behalf of their constituents. Effective use of these methods depends on the resources available to the committees and the respect for the rules of the game by both the executive and the legislative arms of government. Again, legislative committees in most developing countries have been less effective than the British and US examples cited because of a lack of respect for the established rules of the game (see below).

Legal accountability is normally a feature of a law-based state *(Etat de droit)*. This requires governments to respect the rule of law, based on an independent judiciary. The legal order that is established on this foundation typically has a system of courts, and public officials can be held accountable for their actions before the courts. The role of courts in enforcing accountability varies significantly) among countries, ranging from the existence of a specialised administrative court system in some, notably France, to others with an arrangement where the same common law courts handle all the legal disputes, including those relating to citizens' grievances against public officials. Two factors that affect the salience of legal accountability are the quality of legal institutions and citizens' access to courts, especially in terms of the cost of litigation. Weak legal institutions and expensive legal costs (without a system of free legal service) would render legal accountability virtually ineffective.

The Ombudsman: Whether it is established in a constitution or created by legislation, the Ombudsman serves as the "citizens defender." The Ombudsman receives complaints from citizens, investigates them and makes recommendations on how they can be redressed at no cost to citizens. Since the Ombudsman institution was first established in Sweden in the nineteenth century, it has spread to many countries in both industrialised and developing countries. In general, citizens can send their complaints directly to the Ombudsman, either by mail or by telephone. In a few countries, notably Britain, the Ombudsman is regarded as an extension of parliamentary control of the executive and citizens' complaints are channelled through members of parliament. In all cases, the Ombudsman conducts his investigations at no cost to citizens.

Decentralisation and participation: Accountability in public service can also be enhanced through decentralised structures of government and through participation. The typical situation is when government business is devolved to the local level to be managed by local officials who are directly accountable to the local population. As is the case at the central government level, electoral legitimacy is a key factor. However, the extent of accountable behaviour within decentralised government structures is a function of the autonomy of the district and local governments. This varies significantly, ranging from situations of significant autonomy, e.g. US local governments, to limited autonomy, e.g. most developing countries. The increasing reliance on NGOs and community-based organisations and co-operatives in the delivery of public services has emerged as a promising dimension to accountable decentralised public management.

Internal administrative controls: Appointed public officials often play a dominant role in the conduct of government business because of the permanence of their tenure and their technical expertise. Usually, the political heads of government ministries and departments – ministers – are expected to maintain hierarchical control of the officials, with the support of administrative and financial rules and regulations and systems of inspection. In countries with weak administrative structures, notably those in many developing countries and several of the post-communist states, these methods of control have limited impact. This problem is due, in part, to the ambiguous relationship between temporary political leaders and the permanent appointed officials. When they collude, accountability is unattainable (this also happens from time to time in developed countries) and when they are in conflict it almost always results in the phenomenon of two elephants fighting with the general public cast in the role of the grass that suffers.

Mass media and public opinion: In practically every context, the effectiveness of the different methods of enforcing accountability reviewed above depends significantly on whether or not they are supported by a virile mass media and an alert public opinion. To what extent do citizens make use of the available methods and does the mass media give publicity to the abuse of power and to the punishment of abusers? Three factors determine the actual impact of the mass media and public opinion. First, freedom of expression and freedom of association have to be accepted and respected. In many countries, these freedoms are enshrined in constitutional texts. The degree of acceptance and respect can usually be measured by the role of the mass media (including attention to the pattern of ownership) and the vitality of interest groups, trade unions, women's organisations, consumer organisations, co-operatives and professional associations. Second, the conduct of government business must be transparent. The key factor here is citizen access to information. This should preferably be guaranteed by legislation (a "freedom of information act"), excluding only matters relating to state security (in a very narrow sense) and individual privacy. Information generated by governments to which there should be easy access would include budgets, public accounts and audit reports. Without access to information, citizens would be unaware of the acts of omission and commission of governments and the effectiveness of the mass media would be severely limited. The third condition is the civic education of citizens, their understanding of their rights and duties, and their readiness to act accordingly.

The media has a significant role in relation to promoting the accountability of the executive branch of government; in relation to the vibrancy of civil society, itself a vital component of democracies; in facilitating public service reform and helping explain economic transformation; and in scrutinising the functioning of legislatures and the judiciary.

However, there can be obstacles to the effective media performance. These obstacles include:

- legal constraints on the provision or disclosure of official information;
- self-censorship by intimidated journalists;
- political and economic influences on media institutions (often related to concentration of their ownership in relatively few corporate hands);
- hostility of ministers, other politicians and senior civil servants towards the media and towards disclosures of information;
- lack of skills on their part in giving interviews and in dealing with the press;
- corrupt practices by ill-remunerated journalists, accepting money in return for coverage or particular story-lines being run;

- poor conditions of employment of journalists and other media professionals and limitations of available equipment;
- limited resources for pre-and in-service training of media professionals and spokespersons;
- public illiteracy, poverty and physical or logistical constraints on newspaper distribution or broadcast transmission. These obstacles have a negative impact on the promotion of governance in that systems and instruments of accountability have serious limitations. The public, therefore, becomes unaware of how the state is managing the economic and social resources of the country and how power is exercised. The limitations generally prevail in one-party states and military dictatorships whose legitimacy is not sustained by a democratic society.

The next section is devoted to recent trends in Sub-Saharan Africa in respect of the presence or absence of the various methods of enforcing accountability in public service and the actual impact that existing methods have in different countries.

RECENT TRENDS IN SUB-SAHARAN AFRICA

According to a recent press report, President Yoweri Museveni of Uganda has indicated his readiness to "impose on his own government far greater emphasis on transparency and accountability than previously required by multilateral institutions. This would be done to ensure that corruption and politically self-serving policies are monitored by independent auditors and accountants reporting to the major lending organisations."[3] Although Uganda's tough approach to the enforcement of accountability has not yet become widespread in SSA countries, developments in the last six years represent some improvement on previous performance in many cases. (The comprehensive programme on enhancing transparency and accountability that was adopted in Uganda in December 1994 is summarised in Box 1).

The major factor that has pushed accountability to centre stage in SSA in the last six years is the advent of a new political order, emphasis on both electoral

---

[3]   See *Financial Times* (London), February 24–25, 1996: W. Cash, "Move to help Ugandan debt," a "letter to the editor".

legitimacy[4] and a law-based state. By the end of the decade of the 1980s, only a few SSA countries – Botswana, Gambia, Mauritius, Senegal and Zimbabwe – had governments that enjoyed electoral legitimacy, that is with mandates derived from periodic open, free and fair competitive elections. During the first six years of the 1990s, competitive elections had virtually become the norm in the region and more than half of the governments in the region had newly elected presidents or prime ministers, including Benin, Cape Verde, Ethiopia, Lesotho, Madagascar, Malawi, Mali Mozambique, Namibia, and Tanzania. South Africa and Zambia. Elected legislative bodies have also emerged in these countries and parliamentarians in a few countries actually try to provide effective oversight of the executive (for example, Benin, Namibia, South Africa and Zambia). In particular, South Africa is demonstrating strong commitment to respect for proper parliamentary procedures and there is evidence that parliamentary control of the executive is already having some impact. The latest development is that a few of the countries are making progress towards the consolidation of democratic governance by successfully conducting a second series of free and fair competitive elections (Benin, Cape Verde. and Namibia). However, there are some notable exceptions: countries where the results of elections were either annulled (Nigeria, 1993) or rejected (Angola 1993) or – where civil war, civil strife or rebellion made it impossible to organise elections (Liberia, Rwanda, Somalia, Sudan and Zaire). In some of the countries where political accountability has helped to assure political stability, economic policies have become more credible and stable (for example, Benin, Ghana and Uganda) and bilateral and multilateral donors are providing increased development assistance. (In Botswana and Mauritius where the political order has consistently assured stable policies, economic performance has also been good).

---

4   Although traditional legitimacy still enjoys varying degrees of influence in some SSA countries, it is not formally recognised by governments. SSA governments are generally ambivalent in their attitude toward traditional authorities (for example, Nigeria and Senegal). In Botswana, an interesting accommodation between state power-holders and traditional authorities has been achieved in the areas of the administration of justice and land management (M. Dia, 1996: 105–111).

Uganda – Programme on Enhancing Transparency and Accountability: Plan of Action for 1995

1. Awareness
- Seminar/workshops to enhance ethics, transparency and accountability among (i) ministers, permanent secretaries and chief accounting officers; (ii) district government staff; and (iii) judiciary, magistrates, police prosecutors, state attorneys and prison officials.
- Publication of information materials for public servants on corruption, including leadership code and multimedia information for the public.
- Promotion of civil education on the responsibilities of the individual, e.g. anti-corruption week.
- Promotion of civil society, e.g. NGOs, professional groups and interest groups.

2. Preventive Measures
- Simplify management procedures through reduction of red tape.
- Prepare for and monitor effective declaration of assets by key decision-makers.
- Effective prosecution and publication of conviction of serious corruption cases to serve as deterrents.

3. Enforcement
- Organise a special court to handle serious corruption and fraud cases.
- Expedite outstanding serious corruption and fraud cases.
- Establish mechanism for random checking to ensure compliance with regulations by public servants.
- Review and propose strengthened laws relating to corruption, including provision for the freezing, seizing and confiscation of the proceeds of corruption and fraud (including the international elements).
- Enforce the Prevention of Corruption Act of 1970, taking advantage of provisions that shift the burden of proof to accused persons.
- Ensure that books of accounts in ministries and districts are completed by March 1995.

4. Institution Building
- Strengthen relevant agencies such as the Office of the Inspector General of Government, Office of the Auditor General, the Uganda Revenue Authority and Inspectorates in ministries.
- Establish a desk in the office of the IGG to co-ordinate the programme.

Source: Economic Development Institute of the World Bank, Report on a Workshop on Designing a Programme to Enhance Ethics, Transparency and Accountability. Uganda, 9–10 December, 1994.

The emphasis on a law-based state that is a feature of the emerging political order of the 1990s is proving more conducive to the enhancement of legal accountability than the formalistic acceptance of the rule of law adopted in the post-independence constitution of most of the countries. There is a trend towards greater respect for the independence of the judiciary (for example, Benin, Malawi and Zambia) and the imperative of a market economy embraced by virtually every country dictates the strengthening of legal frameworks to ensure the enforcement of contracts and the protection of property. However, legal institutions remain weak in many SSA countries, partly because of inadequately qualified staff and partly because of limited financial resources to build and equip courts. To tackle these problems, several countries are benefiting from the support of multilateral and bilateral donors (for example, Angola, Mozambique, Mali Tanzania and Zambia). Other problems that need to be addressed include consistent enforcement of legal decisions, citizens' limited access to courts and conflicts between "modern" state laws and customary laws.[5]

Normally, the growing independence of both legislative bodies and the courts, made possible by the political pluralism, should help to enhance financial accountability. This is happening only slowly and more at the level of improved legal frameworks such as the recognition of the independence of auditors (Malawi and Uganda) than in practical terms of timely and comprehensive quality audits. Backlogs in audit reports in some countries range from three to over twelve years (for example, Gambia and Nigeria).[6] Public Accounts Committees in the Anglophone countries are still not very effective because the necessary parliamentary culture has not been internalised (e.g. Kenya) and the *cours des comptes* in Francophone countries lack the competence and integrity associated with the French model. A major problem in most of the countries is the inadequacy of qualified professional accountants and auditors, exacerbated by the inability of the public sector to compete with the private sector in attracting and retaining available professionals. A significant increase in the supply of accountants and auditors is the obvious

---

5   Botswana provides a good illustration of genuine effort to "reconcile" modern state law and customary law. See M. Dia, *ibid.*

6   The satisfactory performance of Namibia's Auditor General's Office deserves to be acknowledged. According to a recent study, the Auditor General's reports are "comprehensive, informative, timely, impartial and widely shared." See World Bank, Namibia, *Public Expenditure Review,* Report No. 13558-NAM, July 1995. Botswana and Zimbabwe are also acknowledged to be in the same league as Namibia.

solution. Several countries are benefiting from donor support in this area and some of the donor support is extended to the strengthening of the Offices of Accountants General and Auditors General (for example, Mauritania and Tanzania). The fact that the trained professionals would also be expected to perform at the level of international accounting and auditing standards means that it would take some years for the efforts to have any real impact on financial accountability.

Another important feature of the emerging political order is the empowerment of citizens directly to seek to enforce accountability through the institution of the Ombudsman, through decentralised development management, and through mechanisms of participation. Countries in sub-Saharan Africa with Ombudsman institutions increased from six in 1989[7] to about a dozen in 1995. Recent additions include Malawi, Namibia, Senegal and South Africa. Uganda's Inspector General of Government has a role similar in some respects to that of an Ombudsman. Predictably, the contributions of Ombudsmen to the enforcement of accountability vary from one country to another but in every case, the existence of an Ombudsman is an affirmation of a commitment to assisting citizens who seek redress against maladministration. Suggestions for improving the performance of the Ombudsmen in the region include support for better data management including computerisation) and networking among national Ombudsmen institutions to share experiences and generally support one another (Ayeni, 1993).

The decentralised arrangement that is most conducive to accountable local governance is when the central government devolves power to local governments, thereby constituting them into self-governing institutions with decision-making powers. This helps to enhance the accountability of local officials to the local population as economic and social policies become more responsive to local concerns. Elected local authorities or district assemblies are functioning in Botswana, Ghana, Uganda, Zambia and Zimbabwe. Although the electoral mandate of the locally elected officials would tend to make them accountable to the local population, the overall impact is limited because the scope of local decision-making is constrained by central control. In particular, most local and district governments have to cope with inadequate resources (staff and finance) which leads to a mismatch of resources and responsibilities. Some SSA countries have also adopted the broad interpretation of decentralisation that covers the delegation by central government to private sector entities for the provision of local goods and services. A good illustration

---

[7]   The six countries are: Tanzania, Ghana, Zambia, Sudan, Nigeria and Zimbabwe.

is the AGETIP (*Agence d'Exécution des Travaux d'Intérêt Public*) in which small contractors undertake public works and employment projects financed by governments and/or aid donors in several Francophone African countries, including Senegal, Burkina Faso and Chad. AGETIPs are characterised by considerable participation, improved service delivery and a manifest and impressive degree of accountability.

The emphasis on worldwide participatory development by the donor community, (referred to as people-centred development, PCD) is already having some impact in several SSA countries. It enhances accountability in service delivery because it promotes "a process through which stakeholders influence and share control over development initiatives, and the decisions and resources which affect them" (World Bank, 1996). One approach is citizen representation on administrative boards and agencies, which helps to ensure that the agencies are accountable to local communities (for example village representatives on the national drug procurement agency in Benin (World Bank, 1996: 172). Another approach is the strong support of donors for an increased role for NGOs and community-based organisations in managing development projects throughout the SSA region. The objective is to achieve service delivery at levels closest to the population, thereby ensuring greater accountability. The World Bank is vigorously pushing the NGO approach through the appointment of an NGO liaison officer in each of its Resident Missions throughout the region (since late 1995). The Commonwealth has had an NGO liaison officer for many years.

Regarding internal administrative controls, the general weakness of these methods that was noticeable in the 1960s through the 1970s to the 1980s has persisted. The politicisation of civil service systems that was a major explanatory factor remains a problem in the form of a politics/administration nexus where the respective roles of elected and appointed officials are poorly defined and relationships are characterised by a low trust culture and conflict of varying degrees of intensity. These conflicts have negative consequences for administrative efficiency and fiscal discipline (for example, Benin, Niger, Malawi and Zambia). Efforts aimed at improving personnel and financial management systems (as part of on-going civil service reform programmes in many countries) have not yet produced the expected changes in the attitudes of officials.

AGETIP Experience

AGETIP, *Agence d'Exécution des Travaux d'Intérêt,* a private, non-profit company, was created in Senegal in 1990 in the context of a Public Works and Employment Project. It undertakes "general contracting" of small-scale infrastructure projects financed by IDA, other aid donors, and the Government's own budget. It prepares bidding documents; issues calls for bids; evaluates and awards the bids; signs contracts with winning bidders – usually small-scale contractors; supervises, evaluates, and pays the contractors; and hands the works over to the agencies concerned for operations and maintenance. Overall, there is real competition and transparency in procurement and the entire process is completed in weeks, not months or years. AGETIPs are subject to quarterly audits (by independent external auditors) for the first six months, and twice-yearly thereafter. Payments to contractors are normally made within a few days and rarely exceed a fortnight.

AGETIP Sénégal has implemented 330 projects for a total amount of nearly US$55 million and has created more than 50,000 temporary jobs. By 1993, similar projects had been launched in Niger, Benin, The Gambia, Burkina Faso, Mali and Mauritania. New AGETIPs are in preparation in Guinea, Chad, Madagascar, Togo and Central African Republic.

By facilitating access to the public market and requiring labour-intensive projects, AGETIPs induce local firms to strengthen their competitiveness without endangering employment. This should not only preserve or create new jobs, but also increase firms' profit and therefore fiscal resources, enabling local institutions to finance the maintenance of the works in the medium term and thus trigger sustainable growth. The impact of AGETIPs on institutional development has been positive: the successful use of private sector management techniques in the execution of projects; the emphasis on transparency and accountability; and the impressive record of results achieved in the delivery of services. AGETIPs develop a system of grassroots participation and foster a local sense of project ownership, which is essential for ensuring long-term maintenance.

Today, an increasing number of public authorities are inspired by the AGETIP approach to restructure some government functions to make them more responsive to citizens. Another important development is the promotion of twinning arrangements among AGETIP-type agencies in the Sahel countries as a cost-effective way of building capacity.

Notwithstanding some of the positive developments highlighted above, public accountability remains weak in SSA countries. One notable index of weak accountability is the problem of corruption, especially the phenomenon of unpunished corruption that is rampant in most SSA countries. [8] In many cases, elected and appointed officials collude (sometimes with businessmen as associates) and since external control measures are weak (parliamentary control and judicial control) and with internal controls already by-passed, no sanctions are enforced and corrupt practices increase in scope, becoming institutionalised in a few extreme cases (for example, Nigeria and Zaire). While a few countries launched anti-corruption campaigns in the 1960s and 1970s (notably Tanzania), more widespread anti-corruption efforts started only in the last few years. This development is part of a worldwide trend towards reduced tolerance for corruption, a trend assisted by the publicity given to the exposure of corrupt practices in both developed and developing countries, including Brazil, Britain, France, India, Italy, Kenya, Madagascar, New Zealand, Nigeria, and Zambia.

Uganda is in the forefront of the fight against corruption in SSA (see Box 1). Botswana, Ghana and South Africa are also making serious efforts to curb corruption. (The Botswana effort is summarised in Box on p 58).

Anti-corruption agencies have been established in some countries (Ghana and Malawi) and some have also adopted codes of ethics (conduct), with emphasis on curbing corruption. However, it is not yet clear whether the leadership in these countries has the political will to ensure the effective functioning of these anti-corruption instruments: provision of adequate funding, qualified and independent staff and enforcement of exemplary sanctions ("frying big fishes"). A significant development is the fact that several SSA countries (including Benin, Ghana, Malawi, Mali, Namibia, Tanzania and Uganda) are receiving the assistance of Transparency International (an international NGO leading anti-corruption crusades focused largely on international trade)[9] in

---

[8]   One notable example of punished corruption is from Zimbabwe where an enquiry or corrupt practices led to the resignation of some ministers. See S. T. Agere, "Promotion of good ethical standards in public services in Africa: the case of Zimbabwe," in S. Rasheed and D. Olowu (eds), Ethics and accountability in African public services, Nairobi, ICIPE Science Press, 1993, 147–163.

[9]   On the salience of corrupt practices through international trade, see "Trading on brides," an editorial comment in *The Washington Post* (Washington, D.C.,

Botswana – Curbing Corruption

Directorate on Corruption and Economic Crimes: Although Botswana enjoys the reputation of being one of the few African countries with an honest government, the revelation of several cases of corruption and economic crime in the last few years convinced the government of the need for an anti-corruption campaign.[10] The corruption cases uncovered through public inquiries related to land deals, award of tenders, allocation of houses and contracts for the supply of spare parts and maintenance of vehicles. Several other cases on misappropriation, embezzlement and fraud were uncovered in the 1994 report of the Auditor General. Extensive investigations were conducted in all these cases and disciplinary actions were taken where appropriate. It was against this background that the Corruption and Economic Crime Act of 1994 was passed and a Directorate to investigate and prosecute corrupt officials and businessmen was established in the Office of the President.

A core group of investigators was recruited from Scotland Yard, London Metropolitan Police in England and the Independent Commission against Corruption in Hong Kong. The mandate of the Directorate on Corruption and Economic Crime is to investigate cases and prosecute culprits and to provide public education and prevention. The Directorate has already recorded a spectacular case involving the prosecution of a Bank Manager accused of laundering funds close to P12 million. In 1995, the Director identified the goals of his Directorate as follows: "Our target therefore is a change of attitude amongst the people of Botswana. We must aim to establish a belief that corruption and economic crime cannot be tolerated in a decent democracy such as Botswana but further that those who are guilty of these offices must be caught and punished.

fighting some aspects of corruption. There is strong evidence that corruption undermines development efforts. One illustration is the linkage between aid effectiveness and corruption, which has become a regular discussion topic in meetings on development assistance (Consultative Group meetings and Round

---

March 10, 1996 and "Ending trade corruption," an editorial comment in *Financial Times* (London), March 8, 1996.

[10]   Source: M. Modisi, "Civil Service Reform Experience in Botswana since the 1980s: Lessons of Experience", paper presented at Workshop on Civil Service Reform for Francophone African Countries, Abidjan, January 23–26, 1996.

Tables) since 1992.[11] Since a significant proportion of public spending in SSA countries is derived from development assistance, the linkage is part of the explanation for the increased attention paid to the fight against corruption. Another illustration is the negative impact of systemic corruption on economic and social development in Nigeria: with government revenue of about US$200 billion between 1973 and 1995 (and another US$ 3 billion loan from the World bank), overall economic performance was poor, social development indicators are among the poorest and poverty has increased (World Bank, 1996a).

Where corruption is endemic, it is the means to winning and maintaining the benefits of power. Corruption can infiltrate every aspect of government. An understanding of corrupted power systems may be necessary to re-assess democratic integrity. Answers will not be found in political will or anticorruption commissions alone. Action needs to be pursued in all development activities, as well as in specific anti-corruption measures.

Key outputs could include:

- Transparent mechanisms for political funding
- Appropriate levels of regulation
- Performance management and pay policy in public services
- Transparency in government policy and use of resources
- Independent audit functions
- Parliamentary oversight of standards and conduct
- Systems to respond to citizens complaints
- Detection and punishment of corruption at all levels
- Systems of national and international commercial and criminal law to deter corruption and encourage investment. (DFID paper (unpublished), Feb. 1999.)

Finally, the growing tolerance of diversity in the mass media in most countries with the emergence of independent newspapers and magazines (for example, Benin, Malawi, Mali, Uganda, Zambia) would help the fight against corruption and enhance the use of the other methods of enforcing accountability. The publicity provided in the press is a check on the abuse of power and this is having some impact in some countries (Botswana, Namibia, Kenya, Zambia and South Africa). Equally significant is the fact that the press in some

---

[11]   The problem of corruption features prominently in two recent World Bank publications (World Bank, 1992 and 1994). A proposed "anti-corruption strategy" in the 1994 publication is provided as an Appendix.

countries is undertaking investigative journalism and using it to comment on both the conduct of public officials and the quality, (or lack thereof) of public services in a manner that was unthinkable in the 1980s (Benin, Malawi, Mali and Zambia). However, the mass media remains underdeveloped in some countries (including Cote d'Ivoire and Guinea) and there is evidence of restrictions on restrictions on freedom of the press in a few others (for example, Nigeria and Sierra Leone).

IMPLICATIONS FOR TRAINING

Perhaps the most important conclusion from the review of the methods of enforcing accountability in public service is the extent to which their effectiveness depends on demand. For example, electoral mandates can only meaningfully enhance accountability when citizens use the power of the vote in an enlightened and discriminating manner: to reward good performers and to sanction poor performers. The key issue here is the education of the public, the civic education that enables the average citizen to link his/her vote to the demand for accountability. Civic education is also essential for the enforcement of the other methods of accountability. The low literacy rate in many SSA countries suggests that civic education is low and it would be logical to conclude that overall demand for accountability would be low. The remedy is to increase investment in education. It is also important to mention that political parties and associations of civil society can educate their members on the importance of demanding accountability. In addition, the parties are likely to advise their members to use the other available methods of accountability such as the courts and the Ombudsman. A good test of all educated public demanding accountability would be when individual citizens can use a mix of "voice", "exit" and "control" options to demand it at the level of the provision of specific public services (Paul, 1992).

If improved education for the general public contributes to the demand for accountability, education and training programmes for public officials that emphasise accountability issues have the potential of enhancing both the demand and supply of accountability. Therefore, it is desirable that schools, departments and institutes that provide management training for public officials pay more attention to accountability issues in their training programmes. Besides the training modules[12] that would be available in these institutions, it would also be necessary to develop and run specialised training programmes for the following specific groups who are closely associated with the methods of enforcing accountability: politicians; judicial officials; accountants and auditors; and journalists.

The rather low quality of political leadership in many SSA countries appears to justify the advocacy of carefully tailored education and training programmes for both potential and serving political leaders.[13] A module on accountability issues should feature prominently in such training programmes. If politicians become committed to accountable governance, they will respond both to the demand from citizens for accountable behaviour and they would demand accountability from appointed officials who manage public affairs under their hierarchical control. Training for judicial officials is also needed, both to increase their number and to provide re-training for serving officials to upgrade their knowledge and skills and enable them to exchange views with their colleagues on methods of strengthening judicial control. It is reasonable to expect that increased professionalism among judicial officials would make it more difficult for the executive to "divide and rule" them and this, in turn, will make them better agents for enforcing accountability. Perhaps the most pressing area of need for increased education and training is accounting and auditing. With only a few exceptions, the supply of qualified professionals to undertake accounting and auditing work is inadequate in SSA countries. Again, it is a case of increasing the stock of qualified professionals and up-grading the skills of the qualified personnel, notably in the areas of performance and value-for-money auditing. Finally, there is a huge need to train journalists both in broadening their understanding of political economy and in methods of effective investigation.

---

[12] The contents of such modules (customised for different categories of officials) would reflect both universal ethical values and be a concrete illustration drawn from national and regional realities.

[13] I first joined in this advocacy in my *Politics and Administration in Nigeria* (1986) "Most people will agree that political leaders at all levels of government should possess political and administrative skills and should be imbued with the spirit of public service. The debatable question is whether or not potential and serving political leaders should be subject to formal education and training programmes aimed at preparing them for their leadership roles. For Nigeria and other African states, this question must be answered in the affirmative, and appropriate institutions in each country should assume the responsibility" (p. 187).

The efforts made in the last few years in respect of the training needs identified above have yielded some modest results. For example, parliamentarians in Benin and Kenya who were involved in training in economic management in 1995 stated in the post-training evaluation reports that the experience would improve the quality of their contributions to debates and equip them to work better on parliamentary committees. Several donors are helping to strengthen judicial institutions, notably USAID, UK/ODA and the French Ministry of Co-operation. These bilateral donors as well as the World Bank are also providing support for the training of accountants, auditors and journalists. These training efforts need to be broadened, intensified and sustained both at the national and regional levels.

CONCLUSION

Given the linkage of this regional meeting to the forthcoming Special General Assembly Session on "Public Administration and Development", it is appropriate to conclude this chapter by stressing the fact that concern with accountability in the public service is a worldwide phenomenon. The illustrations of this global concern include, among others, international support for promoting electoral legitimacy, developing and strengthening capacity in judicial administration, accounting and auditing and curbing corruption. The information technology revolution has become a transnational instrument for exposing the worst abuses of the exercise of power, notably in respect of corruption. And it is significant that an international NGO, Transparency International, is leading the fight against corruption in both developed and developing countries.

Towards an Anti-Corruption Strategy

Although such action was not conceived in the first instance as an element in an anti-corruption strategy, the intervention of the World Bank in a number of areas helps countries to control corruption.

The first four types of action reduced opportunities for rent-taking by simplifying rules and by replacing administrative with market with mechanisms:

- Trade regime reforms, which limit the scope for discretionary treatment by customs officials and replace administrative action with price mechanisms in the allocation of import licences arid foreign exchange.

- Tax reform based on lower, uniform rates and simpler rules and the strengthening of tax administration and record-keeping.

- Regulation reform, such as the abolition of price controls, the simplification of license requirements, and similar measures.

- Privatisation, to reduce the size of the state enterprise sector under bureaucratic control.

The next three actions are examples of institutional strengthening to improve controls and reduce incentives for corrupt behaviour.

- Civil service reform, to restore a professional, accountable, realistically paid, and well-motivated bureaucracy.

- Strengthening public procurement systems through the reform of laws, more transparent procedures, adoption of improved bidding documentation, competitive bidding, and staff training.

- Modernisation of public sector accounting, upgrading internal auditing capacity, and strengthening the supreme audit institution.

The agenda could be broadened to include a research programme aimed at better understanding of: (i) the framework of economic incentives for corrupt behaviour; (ii) whether some kinds of corruption are more dysfunctional than others; (iii) the relationship between corruption and political systems; (iv) best practice in countries that have succeeded in curbing corruption; (v) measures that industrialised countries that could take to discourage corrupt practices by exporters. In addition, the World Bank should maintain a dialogue with watchdog organisations established to fight corruption and with governments seeking practical ways to reduce the moral and economic costs of corruption.

Source: World Bank, 1994 *Government: The World Bank Experience*. Washington D.C., p 16.

REFERENCES

Adamolekun, L. 1974. "Accountability and Control Measures in Public Bureaucracies. A Comparative Analysis of Anglophone and Francophone Africa", *International Review of Administrative Sciences. L,4,307–321*

Adamolekun, L. 1986. *Politics and Administration in Nigeria.* London, Hutchinson.

Anyang Nyong'o. 1993. "Education and Training in Democratic Ethical Values for African Public Services," in S. Rasheed and D. Olowu (eds), *Ethics and Accountability in African Public Services*, Nairobi: ICIPE Science Press, 213–220.

Ayeni, V. 1993. "The Ombudsman's Statistics: on data-gathering and management in the enforcement of public accountability in Africa", *International Review of Administrative Sciences,* 60, 1, 55–70.

Dia, M. 1996. *Africa's Management in the 1990s and Beyond, Reconciling Indigenous and Transplanted Institutions,* Washington, D.C., the World Bank.

Dwivedi, O.P. and D. Olowu (eds), 1988. "Bureaucratic Morality", special issue of *International Political Science Review,* 9,3.

Eigen, P. 1993. "Transparency International – The Coalition against Corruption in International Business Transactions," *Development and Co-operation,* 2,1.

Good, K. 1994. "Corruption and mismanagement in Botswana: A best case example?" *Journal of Modern African Studies,* 32, 3, 499–521.

Johnson S. and J. Makanda. 1996. *Public Sector Financial Management in sub-Saharan Africa*, Draft Technical Paper, Capacity Building and Implementation Division, Africa Technical Department, the World Bank, Washington D.C.

Makanda, J. 1994. *Financial Accountability and Economic Performance, processed.* Capacity Building and Implementation Division, Africa Technical Department, the World Bank, Washington D.C.

Paul, S. 1992. "Accountability in Public Services: Exit, Voice and Control", *World Development*, 20, 7, 1047–1060.

Polidano, C., Why Bureaucrats Can't Always Do What Ministers Want: Multiple Accountabilities in Westminster Democracies. Public Policy and Administration 13, No. 1, Spring 1998, p 38.

Rasheed, S. and D. Olowu (eds). 1993. *Ethics and Accountability in African Public Services*, Nairobi, ICIPE Science Press.

Transparency International (TI). 1995. *A national integrity blueprint. A practical handbook on best practice for the containment of corruption and the building of transparent and accountable government, processed.*

Watson, David: Media and Governance: Concepts and Applications, ed. Joan Corkery: International Institute of Administrative Sciences, 1999, p 208.

World Bank, 1992. *Governance and development,* Washington, D.C.

World Bank, 1994. *Government: the World Bank experience*, Washington, D.C.

World Bank, 1995. *Africa: A Continent in Transition,* Washington, D.C.

World Bank, 1996. *World Bank Sourcebook on Participation,* Washington, D.C.

World Bank, 1996a. *Nigeria – Poverty assessment.* Report No. 14733-UNI, West Africa Department.

PUBLIC AND PRIVATE SECTOR PARTNERSHIP/PARADIGM

INTRODUCTION

The debate about the need to develop an appropriate development paradigm with its requisite structures and systems has been the subject of public administration scholars, policy-makers, managers and the consumers of services for many decades. The central question that has always been raised in this debate is the typology of quantity and quality of the relationship between the public and private sector in the development process.

PUBLIC AND PRIVATE SECTOR PARTNERSHIP IN GOVERNANCE

Governance, the exercise of political, economic and administrative authority in the management of a country's affairs, is a concept which comprises the complex mechanisms, processes, relationships and institutions through which citizens and groups articulate their interests, exercise their rights and obligations and mediate their differences. Good governance therefore addresses the allocation and management of resources to respond to collective problems; it is characterised by participation, transparency, accountability, rule of law, effectiveness and equity.

Governance includes the state, but transcends it by taking in the private sector and civil society. All three are critical for sustaining human development. The state creates a conducive political and legal environment. The private sector generates jobs and income; civil society facilitates political and social interaction – mobilising groups to participate in economic, social and political activities (UNDP).[1]

The public and private sector interface, therefore, seeks to promote constructive debate, focus and meaningful interaction of all the three actors in governance. It is hoped that such an interaction of critical actors will not only facilitate the development process but will also ensure the efficient and effective delivery of service to people, including the poorest of the poor, who often do not have access to services such as education, health etc. Improving service delivery to the poor should also become a focus for both the public and private sectors as they all stand to benefit from the development of human resources.

TRENDS IN DEVELOPMENT PARADIGMS

There are various development paradigms that have been dominant at a particular phase in the development history of most of the developing Commonwealth states since independence. For ease of reference they are set out below:

- When most governments gained independence, it was assumed that the private sector, left to itself, would neither generate nor allocate investment resources optimally and that government would have to take the lead role in guiding the transformation of the economies.

- In pursuit of this development paradigm, many governments nationalised certain enterprises and new state-owned enterprises were created. The countries implemented import substitution protectionist policies, which included maintenance of over-valued exchange rates, and imposition of high tariff and barriers to imports. This paradigm had a bias against exports, the largest suppliers of foreign exchange.

- The poor performance in the 1980s of most of the Commonwealth's developing economies led to changing perceptions of economic policies and development paradigms. The private sector was then recognised as the engine for development and growth while the public sector was recognised as the facilitator for growth. Partnership between the public and private sector, therefore, became the main focus of debate. The role of the state was to be redefined in line with the assumptions of the lead role of the private sector and of its role of being a facilitator.

- The parameters of the globalisation process assume that the public sector is central to economic and social development, not as a direct provider of growth but as a partner, catalyst and facilitator. The renewed call for partnership between these two sectors in the development process is now advocated by many donors, international financial institutions and many of the aid recipient countries.

In addition to public and private sector partnership, the recent wave of globalisation of the Eighties and Nineties, has been driven by a new set of factors such as deregulation, in particular, of financial services, emergence of new transportation and communication technologies, collapse of the eastern bloc and the demonstration effect of the success stories of the East Asian economies often referred to as East Asian miracles or tigers and public sector reforms. While the theoretical assumptions have not been analysed nor the dominant forces in the paradigm rigorously examined, suffice it to say that the basis for all these changes can be categorised as follows:

First, they are a direct result of globalisation forces and processes or, metaphorically, the winds of change once coined by Harold McMillan former Prime Minister of Britain.

Secondly, the evidence of poor performance of the economy, poor management by the state and poor but inadequate delivery of service to consumers and society as a whole.

Thirdly, and as a consequence of the above, the quest to find better methods, practices and systems of improving the delivery of service amidst the growing dissatisfaction of the public on the performance of the state.

CONCEPT OF PARTNERSHIP

The debate on the essence of the public/private sector partnership is not new to development economics or to the management of policies formulated by the state. It has always aimed at finding possible ways of managing the economy and improving the delivery of service to the public and consumers. It has, therefore, been used as an instrument, either for change or for continuity, in dealing with issues and problems. It has always been assumed that the symbiosis of the public and private sector, in the right proportion, might improve the management of the economy.

Defining the concept of partnership can be a problem in the sense that it brings different meanings to different people. In this regard, we shall define partnership as a framework of policies, practices, procedures and assumptions that provide guidance for managing the economy and for improving the process of development.

Partnership for development is an agreement negotiated by the state and the social partners, namely the private sector institutions. It represents a strategic approach to leading the economy and society into the 21st century. The objectives may be continued development of an efficient economy capable of economic growth and operating within the constraints of the globalisation process. The aim is to make society more inclusive, reduce long-term unemployment, and ensure that the benefits of growth are more equally distributed. Partnership can, in certain circumstances, be similar to the social construction of bridges between partners in development in order to compare the delivery of service to the consumers.

Defined in this way, partnership is not a new concept. It has always been concerned with determining the appropriate means of defining sets of working relationships that are meaningful and productive. The formal relationship focuses on the development and management of human, financial and material resources in order to produce a viable economy.

The Asian Development Bank states that:

> "The manner in which the public and private sectors function together in an economy is one test of the effectiveness of the participation/partnership principle. From the point of view of economic growth and development, this interface can work at two levels. First, market-friendly economic reforms (i.e. a conducive environment for private enterprise) help release the energies and dynamism of the private sector and enable it to contribute more fully to the development process (thus making it more broad-based and participatory). Second, consultative mechanisms for dialogue between government and private actors (e.g. business councils) can give the latter opportunities to provide effective input into the policy process. Such business councils can be valuable to the government as well. By including the relevant parties in the discussion, they increase the government's capacity to achieve consensus on policy initiatives. Other advantages include enhanced credibility of the government's commitment to growth, and increased safeguards against corruption."[2]

These consultative mechanisms, designed properly, have a potential to increase not only participation and accountability as discussed earlier, but also transparency and predictability in policy formulation and implementation. Such an open relationship and shared commitment contribute to the promotion and improvement of good governance.

At the least, a partnership suggests mutual contribution – financial, institutional, and intellectual – with shared objectives, decision-making and benefits, however, the public-private partnership is a unique relationship in that it balances the competing and sometimes incompatible objectives of public interests and private enterprise. The relationship also shows how to maximise scarce resources and avoid duplication of effort in the delivery of services to the public at least cost to the taxpayer.

In some countries, the public and private sector environment is overshadowed by declining levels of trust and confidence in the political leaders and public institutions and a public that is demanding faster, more convenient and more responsive service delivery and which is extremely vocal and critical of the government's ability to meet their evolving needs. The public service, in particular, is being criticised daily about the way the service is delivered.

Based on these complaints and criticisms, the public sector is under pressure to find ways of resolving the problems. One such possible way is to form partnerships with many stakeholders in society and together formulate solutions. Such a strategy, which is internally owned and driven, has a more chance of success than the one imposed externally.

Citizen trust in government is important to public administrators because it is central to citizen support for the creation and implementation of public policies, and subsequently, for effective co-operative compliance. Ellram (1995) defines partnership as "an ongoing relationship between two organisations which involves a commitment over an extended time period, and a mutual sharing of the risks and rewards of the relationship.[3] Ellram further states that it is not unusual to describe a partnership as an alliance, or strategic alliance, where the parties bring together apparently complementary skills to exploit an opportunity that neither wishes to pursue on their own.

The advantages of partnerships are found in the competitive edge and benefit from the mutual dependency or trading partners that arise from the management advantages of working with partner organisations which have a mutual understanding of each other's culture and strategic intent, including compatibility between top management team of both organisations.

Three success factors can be identified in partnership and these are partner contribution, personnel and financial issues and interactions. These factors assume that each partner will add value to the relationship, that there will be an environment of trust and mutual, open exchange of information and ideas between the individuals directly involved.

In a development perspective, partnership is not just a relationship between two partners but also among many partners. In development terms, partnership can be used synonymously with technical co-operation. In development projects, for example, partnership can include non-government organisations both national and local, government bodies, donors, multilateral and bilateral agencies, church organisations and community-based organisations. The success of partnership between and among agencies and the public sector depends on the manner in which it is perceived. For example, as a channel for resources; as a way of working and co-operating; or as a vehicle for developing a fairer relationship between them. However, a lasting partnership must be based on mutual trust and respect, to see in the other's experience an enrichment of one's own. Partnership in development can also be forged in different sectors of the economy, such as health, education, and rural development as well as in the poor sections of society.

COMPOSITION OF PARTNERSHIP AND KEY ACTORS

In general, partnership comprises various forces, some of which are more powerful than others while some may be unequal to others, both in the determination of policies and the ownership of resources. Partnerships, like globalisation, are dictated by certain circumstances, episodes and forces in society. The nature and type of partnership is therefore determined by historical circumstances and problem-solving mechanisms.

In partnerships such as occur in the globalisation process, a number of questions, issues and concerns arise. The questions generally concern the composition, nature and typology of partnership. Who decides, for example, about the form of partnership? What kind of partnership can be developed between and among unequal partners with unequal access and opportunities to resource and decision-making powers? Is there such a thing as equal partnership? These questions and more are pertinent in understanding the composition of partnership.

In the globalisation process, at present, the global economic governance is dominated by the G7 countries and the Bretton Woods institutions. The G7 is highly restricted in its membership; and the voting structures in the World Bank and IMF reinforce the asymmetry in global economic decision-making.

The composition of the G7 and the voting structure within the Bretton Woods institutions render the current system unsatisfactory. The democratic deficit built into its workings reduces its legitimacy.[4]

If this is the case, a question must be asked: what kind of globalisation can we expect from partners between industrial, emerging and developing countries? The questions that are asked in the globalisation process are also pertinent to issues of partnership between nation states and between the public and private sector in any one country.

In building a partnership framework within a country the following questions are generally put forward for consideration:

- What is the percentage of the role of the state in the management of the economy? Should it be 35%, 45% or 55%?

- What is the optimal mix?

- Where are global interests placed?

There is no single answer to these questions. However, I believe that a consensus can be built up by the appropriate partners on the right type of optimal mix and on the role of the state. What is important is to identify a modality of reaching an agreement between the participating partners and civil society.

There are three key actors that appear to be appropriate in forging a partnership in development and delivering service to the people. These three actors are the state, the private sector and civil society.

The state's functions are to establish and maintain stable, effective and fair, legal-regulatory frameworks for public and private activity. It means ensuring stability and equity in the market place. It means mediating interests for the public good. It also means providing effective and accountable public services. In each of the four roles the state faces a challenge, i.e. ensuring that good governance addresses the concerns and needs of the poorest by increasing the opportunities for people to seek, achieve and sustain the kind of life to which they aspire.[5]

The state can also ensure the upholding of human rights and the maintenance of the stable, macroeconomic conditions necessary for people and institutions to preserve standards, law and order, security and harmony. The state should ensure that there are free and fair elections held periodically and make itself accountable to the public.

The private sector is regarded as an engine for development in that it creates jobs that provide enough income to improve living standards. The state has to ensure that the environment in which the private sector operates is conducive to productivity and increasing investment.

The private sector has social, economic, financial and political roles. One of its social roles, apart from employment creation, is to provide certain services that cannot be provided by government, such as relief services and networking with other productive organisations. Its economic role can be realised in research and development, science and technology, the development of industries, export and import, the mobilisation of resources through shareholders, and exploitation of natural resources. The private sector plays an important financial role in that it is directly involved in banking and insurance, thereby strengthening the financial market. Its political role is exercised through the promotion of international relations, the monitoring of the electoral process and through partnership in promoting transparency and consensus-building in development.

Civil society is the third key actor in the process of developing and maintaining good governance. Civil society connects individuals with the public realm and the state through various interest groups and organisations. Civil society allows the participation of citizens in economic and social activities that have the potential of influencing government in policy development and management. It can provide checks and balances on government power and monitor social abuses.

In Malaysia, for example, developing partnership with industry is seen through the operationalisation of the Malaysian Incorporated Policy, introduced in 1983 as one of the major strategies for national economic growth. This policy requires that public and private sectors see the nation as a corporate or business entity, jointly owned by both sectors and working in tandem in the pursuit of shared corporate goals. Policy implementation can take the form of consultative panels, forums, seminars, workshops, training programmes and even funding.[6]

Partnership with industry is promoted essentially through consultative panels, which must be established in each ministry at the federal state and local district levels. The apex of these consultative panels of officials is chaired by the Chief Secretary to the government, the highest and most senior government official. The members of the panels are captains of industry, representative organisations of the private sector and senior government officials. An important contribution from the private sector is the opportunity given to senior government executives to participate in attachment training programmes in private firms.

THE IMPACT OF PARTNERSHIP IN ORGANISATIONS

Once the type of partnership to be formed has been determined by the stakeholders, the public and private sector instruments that implement the policy will have to be reorganised in such a way that the objectives of the partnership can be achieved. Consequently, the public sector must be restructured so that it can develop the capacity and capability to work with the private sector in the development process.

In a meaningful partnership both the public and private sectors must aim to improve productivity. This means that the public sector must develop a business approach. The performance of the public sector would be expected to be subjected to the same managerial disciplines as the private sector. The public sector, for example, would be expected to improve service quality and test performance, and the traditional notions of accountability would have to change to modern managerialism which emphasises results rather than process and prescription. Within the public sector, accountability is still perceived in terms of compliance or inputs rather than in terms of effective achievements of outcomes.

A more effective and meaningful organisational culture has to be developed. The public sector in particular has to develop mission statements, values and beliefs and to emphasise the need to produce value for customers and stakeholders, as in the private sector. In such circumstances, the objectives of the organisations have to be clearly defined. Corporate planning and corporate culture have to be embedded in the organisations.

There must be efficient human resources management if productivity is to be achieved. Human resources would be held directly accountable for their performance. As in the private sector, rewards for employees could be linked more directly to rewards for performance.

The main ways in which to change the rules of the game, particularly in the public sector, are to form alliances and mergers where appropriate, form customer-supply partnerships and develop ventures that allow pioneering technology and approaches. These changes are essential for the 21st century and corporations will find it hard to survive unless they get better results from their employees and satisfy the public and civil society.

THE GUIDING PRINCIPLES FOR PARTNERSHIP SUSTAINABILITY

For the partnership between the public and private sectors to survive it must be based on certain principles and practices. The following principles are suggested:

- There is a growing recognition that the desirable partnership must be *home-grown*. In other words, the policy must be locally owned with both political commitment and management leadership, be participative, involving clients, workers and unions and, above all, be client-focused and driven by the needs of society. A meaningful partnership cannot be imposed from outside, however powerful the tools of persuasion.

- Strong *leadership and commitment* to achieve the desired partnership are essential if it is to be sustained. There are so many forces resistant to change in public sector organisations that unless the government moves to create sustained pressure for change, resistance will not be overcome.

- There must be a balance between *vision and social reality*. The vision of the society that people want to live in and the vision of the public service that is needed to achieve a society must be clearly articulated. Fundamental questions about the role of the state need to be addressed to achieve this vision and these questions are the ones that ought to be the subject of discussion across political parties, with leaders in the private sector and in the non-government organisations and labour unions.

- It is recognised that pressure to develop partnership needs to be tempered with a *realistic appraisal* of the social consequences. The disparity between the wealthy and the poor should not grow, as the partnership is developed so that the poorest members of society are not subjected to unacceptable living standards and thereby become alienated.

75

- Sustainable partnership needs to be tackled through a *participative approach* that harnesses the knowledge and commitment of a wide variety of interested parties. Granting people the opportunity to play a meaningful part in the overall partnership development is more likely to build consensus and achieve change than limited negotiation on specific issues.

- Organisations are a complex interaction of systems and people. However perfectly designed the systems might be, they will not work effectively if people in the organisation do not have the right combination of *skills, knowledge and attitudes*. It is generally easier to redesign systems than it is to re-equip people, so all too often partnership concentrates on structures, procedures, rules and regulations etc. without placing sufficient emphasis on the human dimension. The human dimension is more than training people to operate new systems; it is about involvement in the determination of the mission and goals of the organisation. It is about involvement in the analysis of the shortcomings of the organisation in its ability to secure its goals, and involvement in policy determination, implementation and evaluation. Training should be fully integrated into human resource management and the responsibility for staff development should be seen as essential for every manager.

- The process of management depends on the availability of *timely and accurate information* and partnership efforts recognise that investment in information technology is essential.

ETHICS IN PARTNERSHIP

In addition to the factors already mentioned, successful partnership also depends on performance management. Performance management incorporates corporate and strategic planning to define the long- and short-term aims and values of an organisation; the translation of the objectives into operational plans for the organisation, divisions and individuals; the assessment and provision of training and other resources based on the priorities identified in the planning phase; the development of appropriate measures of performance at the level of the organisation, the division and the individual; and the regular review, adjustment, feedback and recognition of achievement.

Different work methods are designed to ensure that the tasks and priorities of employees are in alignment with the objectives of the organisations. Work methods also will identify needs in the areas of skills training and career development, and will foster continuous communication, coaching and feedback between supervisors and employees. Performance appraisal systems therefore become critical in performance management.

Performance management systems in the promotion of partnership must be underpinned by high standards of conduct. Ethics is a core element of performance management. Ethical conduct is becoming a major concern of many, both in the public and the private sector. The concern is based on the decline in the level of competence, performance and confidence in public institutions, coupled with corruption and scandals. Ethics is a major issue in the delivery of service to consumers and the public. The designing of a well-functioning ethics infrastructure will encourage high standards of behaviour. The elements of an ethics infrastructure include guidance, management and control. Guidance is provided by strong commitment from the political leadership and the development of codes of conduct and providing employees with education and training. Management can be realised through co-ordination by a special body and the establishment of conditions, management policies and practices that encourage ethical conduct. Conduct is assured principally through a legal framework establishing independent investigation and prosecution; effective accountability and control mechanisms; transparency; and public involvement and scrutiny.

The following are some of the principles for managing ethics as suggested by the International Personnel Management Association.[7]

- Ethical standards should be clear so that employees know the principles and standards they are expected to apply to their work. The code of conduct should be shared with all employees.

- Ethical standards should be reflected in the legal framework, which is the basis for communicating the minimum standards and principles of behaviour for all employees.

- Ethical guidance should be provided to public servants. Training in ethics, so that employees can develop the necessary skills for ethical analysis and moral reasoning, should be encouraged.

- Employees should know their rights and obligations when exposing actual or suspected wrongdoing.

- The political leadership must lead by example: it should promote legislation and regulations reinforcing ethical behaviour and creating sanctions against wrongdoing.

- The decision-making process should be transparent and open to scrutiny with oversight by the legislature and access provided to public information.

- There should be clear guidelines for interaction between public and private sectors in dealing with such issues as procurement and privatisation of public employment.

- Managers should demonstrate and promote ethical conduct. High standards of conduct should be encouraged by providing appropriate incentives for ethical behaviour.

- Management policies, procedures and practices should demonstrate an organisation's commitment to ethical standards.

- Public service employment conditions such as career and personal development, human resources management policies and compensation systems should create an environment that promotes ethical conduct. Basic principles such as merit in recruitment and promotion help to institutionalise integrity in the public service.

- Adequate accountability mechanisms should be in place so that public servants are accountable for their actions to their superiors and ultimately the public. Accountability should focus on both compliance with ethical principles and on the achievement of results.

- Appropriate procedures and sanctions should exist to deal with misconduct. A necessary part of an ethics infrastructure must include ways to detect and investigate allegations of wrongdoing.

Since independence in most of the developing countries, there has been a noticeable increase in poor performance and corruption, and a decline in ethical standards where wrongdoing can be detected and disciplinary measures taken. The poor relationship between the public and private sectors, the mistrust and suspicion between them has even become a problem in building partnerships and bridges in the development process.

The socio-economic and political environment is overshadowed by the declining levels of trust and confidence in political leadership and public institutions, and a the public which is demanding faster, more convenient and more responsive service delivery, and which is extremely vocal and critical of the government's ability to meet its evolving needs. The public service in particular has come under persistent attack and criticism by politicians, consumers and civil society for poor service delivery. This organisational environment has been exacerbated by the deteriorating relationship between politicians or elected officials and civil servants or appointed officials in the management of human and financial resources for the public good. Evidence of the lack of trust and confidence is reported daily in the media.

In the United Kingdom, ethical challenges were at the forefront of public debate at the time when the Committee on Standards in Public Life was formed. Lord Nolan, who was the first Chairman of the United Kingdom Committee on Standards in Public Life, argued that:

> "To meet all these concerns, it is essential that issues of ethics and standards have a high priority in the new public service. There is a need for clear ethical principles to help those who are not by background imbued with public service values. These principles must be framed in such a way that the new manager will understand the importance of them and can integrate them into the managerial structure of the organisation." [8]

At its formation, the Committee set out seven principles of public life and these are selflessness, integrity, accountability, openness, honesty and leadership. The codes of conduct were formulated to ensure that the set standards would be enforced. However, codes of conduct alone may not achieve the desired results unless they are underpinned by the commitment, will and capacity of those who enforce them. The successful enforcement of codes also depends upon a number of factors of which induction and training are part. Induction in ethical matters is particularly important, so that no public servant can claim ignorance of the rules and so that good habits can be instilled before bad ones are learned. Training or induction is necessary for both politicians and civil servants who operate in such organisations. This includes board members, chief executives, and staff. Such training needs are extended to senior management, partly as a way of keeping the management team involved with and supportive of the corporate commitment and partly to encourage them to keep standards alive and relevant. If the standards are to be maintained, they must permeate the organisation from top to bottom and back again.

For as long as anyone cares to remember, we have been mired in a debate over the allocation of resources between the private and public sectors. Whether it is capitalism versus communism, privatisation versus nationalisation, or the markets of business versus controls of government, the arguments have always pitted private, independent forces against public, collective ones.[9]

The public-private sector interface debate has always existed in the historical past in different situations. The debate has taken different forms depending on the size of the government and the private sector. At the centre of the debate, whether in a socialist or capitalist society, government has been the modality and form of working together for the good of society.

Recently, in Malaysia and the South East Asian countries, the smart partnership concept was developed between the state, labour and other sectors in the private sector and key consultative forces in civil society. The objectives of the fora are:

- To create a smart partnership amongst key economic players, namely government, private sector, labour and other stakeholders in order to enhance the economic development process of the nation.

- To provide broad participation in the formation of national economic policy through an interchange of ideas and experiences amongst government, private sector, labour, academia and civil society.

- To facilitate the co-ordination, monitoring and evaluation of national economic policy implementation.

The whole issue of smart partnership is based on the principle that any economy is an integral whole with the general infrastructure, business processes and social responsibilities all feeding into the other. It is about creating limitless opportunities and wealth that is shared, sustainable and allows participants to function in the global economy. Each partner plays a different role according to their different circumstances, but all operate from the same set of principles, practices, ethics and procedures.

The benefits derived from the attempts to integrate into national economies are some of the latest innovations in policy analysis and implementation. Co-ordination and collaboration have been spread by the Commonwealth Secretariat through global, regional and sub-regional workshops.

The forms of partnership might vary from one country to the other but in essence they constitute an attempt to solve economic and social problems. Many governments in the South East Asian region decided to adopt the smart partnership concept, having identified some contradictory factors such as:

- Government commitment to social equity countered by the failure of economic growth, the fall in disposable incomes and growing social unrest.

- The ideological propensity for state intervention, countered by the inability to maintain public sector investment and strong pressures to liberalisation under structural adjustment programmes. Governments, often under pressure from donors as well as from internal forces for change, had to rethink their service provision roles as well as their policy development process. The formation of smart partnerships therefore constitutes an important component of the changing traditional practices in public sector management.

ATTITUDINAL AND BEHAVIOURAL PATTERNS

The success of partnership or smart partnership depends not only on the systems, procedures and practices put in place but also on the right attitudes and behavioural patterns of those who manage and deliver the services. The wrong attitudes exhibited by practitioners will tend to negate all the attempts to make partnership work.

The bureaucratic attitudes based on an outdated Whitehall model and made rigid by legal and constitutional arrangements and outdated administrative systems, are still dominated by rules, regulations and central control which impede the evolution of modern management attitudes and practices to the detriment of the client-oriented partnership concept. Attitudes and behavioural patterns inherited from the colonial past certainly challenge any assumptions that management cultures can easily be imported from North America and Western Europe without modification to the regional or national reality. Governments need, therefore, to identify those behavioural patterns that can impede the development of a meaningful and effective partnership.

Experience has shown that any development paradigm or model needs to be underpinned by correct and appropriate attitudes. Such attitudes as respect for clients, being friendly to consumers of policy, and having the commitment to help, can facilitate the formation of the public-private sector partnership and the delivery of service. The emphasis on authority, seniority etc. to the exclusion of friendly care tends to undermine the whole process of developing a meaningful partnership that can deliver the goods.

In many public services, absenteeism from work is on the increase, favouritism based on gender and ethnicity is growing and, above all, corruption has reached incredible proportions. Poor performance and mismanagement are also on the increase. These negative attitudes adversely affect the successful management of partnership.

What is needed, therefore, is for both the public and private sectors to create a type of partnership that is suitable for the country and to involve all the stakeholders. The partnership must be owned and directed by the stakeholders. While it is good to learn from other countries and organisations, the imposition of development models should be resisted unless they are modified to suit the local socio-economic and political circumstances.

REFERENCES

1. UNDP Governance Policy Paper (1998) unpublished paper.

2. Asian Development Bank: Governance: Sound Development Management. 1995, unpublished paper.

3. Ellram, L. M. (1995), Partnering Pitfalls and Success Factors. International Journal of Purchasing and Materials Management, 31(2): pp 35–44.

4. Public lecture by the Commonwealth Secretary-General, Chief Emeka Anyaoku, at Universiti Sains Malaysia, 27 October 1998.

5. UNDP op cit

6. Commonwealth Secretariat: Current Good Practices and New Developments in Public Service Management: A Profile of the Public

Service of Malaysia. The Public Service Country Profile Series No. 3 1995, p 105.

7. Lord Nolan: Just and Honest Government in Public Administration and Development: The International Journal of Management Research and Practice, ed. Paul Collins, Vol 18 No. 5, December 1998.

8. 23rd International Symposium on Public Personnel Management, Paris, France, April 26–30, 1998.

9. Mintzberg, Henry, Managing Government or Governing Management. Harvard Business Review, May–June 1996, p 76.

THE ROLE OF THE STATE IN CREATING
A CONDUCIVE ENVIRONMENT

At independence, many Commonwealth developing countries believed that political independence by itself was insufficient unless accompanied by economic independence and self-sufficiency. Rapid industrialisation in the domestic economy was considered key to the acceleration of the development process. As a result, it was believed that planning and public ownership constituted key instruments in pushing forward the objectives of political and economic independence.

Development economists argued that the private sector in developing countries lacked the means, both in terms of financial capital and entrepreneurial skills, to undertake the task of development. Citizens expected the newly independent state to deliver the fruits of independence. To meet this expectation, governments were forced to resort to direct intervention in the economy. As a result, planning was considered a vital instrument for capital formation. Domestic resources were required to overcome the saving constraints. In the face of the weak financial markets, government intervention was considered a must. Industrialisation was pursued as a strategy to accelerate development. Protection of infant industries against competition and import substitution constituted the cornerstones of the industrialisation policy.

Apart from the above considerations, concerns with market failures, the rationale of increasing returns to scale, the fear that public and merit goods would not be produced in sufficient quantity if left to the market, questions of fair distribution and elimination of poverty and unemployment as major goals of development, the difficulty of relying on the private sector to ensure balanced regional development, and national security considerations, all provided the rationale for intervention and control in all aspects of the economy. As Mukandala observes, "the public enterprise sector helped to address objectives such as economic nationalism, filling structural gaps, transition to socialism, plums for the elite, modernization of development administration, security and capital cost, minimization for multi-national corporations (MNCs), institutional instincts for self-preservation." (Mukandala, 1988)

After independence in many of the developing Commonwealth countries, three patterns of post-colonial government emerged. The first was the multi-party democracy, the second was the one-party state, and the third was the military government.

National leaders who opted for a one-party state argued that in order to foster national integration for economic and social development, they needed to speak with one voice and could therefore not afford the divisive trends inherent in the opposition parties and confrontational politics. According to this view, a single party structure was the most effective way of harnessing the energies of the people for the purpose of nation-building. The one-party rule was achieved through negotiations and merger, while in other countries it was forced on the opposition through legislation.

While in some cases the one-party rule may have stabilised national politics, it did so at the expense of insulating governments from constructive criticism and by stifling enterprise outside the narrow confines of the political elite. In a one-party state, criticism or self-criticism was supposed to be conducted within the ruling party and not outside.

In still other countries, not long after independence, the military emerged as the government-in-waiting. In nearly all such countries, the military would often seek to justify their takeover of government by pointing to the corruption of the political classes which, they argued, rendered the later right to govern. (Commonwealth Currents 2/97)

However, since 1991, many Commonwealth African states, for example, have moved to establish democratic rule through multi-parties. A number of factors have contributed to the transition to democracy. First, the fall of communism in Eastern Europe and secondly, western creditor governments and international financial institutions reinforced pressures for change. From the early 1980s they began to impose stringent economic conditions on the provision of debt relief and new loans. They then widened conditionality to include transparent administration, the protection of human rights and the restoration of democracy.

Within the Commonwealth, the democratisation process has been strengthened by declarations made by Heads of State at their periodic meetings. The Harare Commonwealth Declaration of 1991, for example, committed Commonwealth members to democracy, the democratic process and institutions which reflect national circumstances, the rule of law and the independence of the judiciary, just and honest government, fundamental human rights, including equal rights and opportunities for all citizens regardless of race, colour, creed or political belief. This commitment was reaffirmed and strengthened in 1995 at Millbrook, New Zealand, where Commonwealth Heads of Government agreed to an Action Programme to fulfil more effectively the commitments contained in the Harare Declaration. This Action Programme was a clear indication that Commonwealth leaders were determined to act on the commitments they had undertaken at Harare (Commonwealth Currents, 1977).

However, the performance of the state and its failure to achieve its developmental promises cast serious doubt on its effectiveness to spearhead the production sector. Rising debt and growing budget deficits forced a thorough look and re-examination of expenditure patterns resulting in cost-consciousness, reluctance to engage in activities that it could not efficiently discharge. There has thus been growing pressure to redefine its role.

THE NEW ROLES OF THE STATE

Proponents of the new role of the state called for a minimalist state. At times it appeared as if the argument was pushed too far. A call for the state's new role did not necessarily imply total abdication of responsibilities. Extreme positions, however, were sometimes taken, calling on the state to leave many of its traditional activities to the private sector. However, such positions were strongly contested. What was needed was not the withering away of a state as such, but rather a consensus seems to be emerging that the existence of a strong state was a crucial prerequisite for the successful development of the private sector and promotion of good governance. This position is eloquently articulated by Klitgaard who observes:

> "In the wake of free market reforms that have spread throughout the world in the past fifteen years...Government remains a principal actor in macroeconomic policy-making infrastructure, and social programs, – not to mention defence, justice, and foreign policy. Successful markets themselves require the highly skilled public management of the privatisation process, new efforts to protect the environment, policies that promote and protect competition and the sophisticated regulation of capital markets, banking systems, and decreasing cost industries. For the institutions of the free market to work, government institutions must also work." (Klitgaard, 1994).

86

In a recent publication, the World Bank identifies five fundamental tasks that lie at the core of a government's mission. These fundamentals have to be in place if a sustainable, shared and poverty-reducing development strategy is to work. These fundamentals include:

- establishing a foundation of law;
- maintaining a non-distortionary policy environment, including macroeconomic stability;
- investing in basic social services and infrastructure;
- protecting the vulnerable;
- protecting the environment; and
- investing.

These fundamentals constitute the major roles that the state is called upon to assume nowadays. The public sector could stimulate, facilitate and support the development of the private sector as well as enhance the linkages between investment, production, trade and technology. Hence, we shall briefly examine what the state, in the framework of its new role, can do to support the efforts of the private sector so that it can serve as an engine of growth.

THE ROLE OF THE PUBLIC SECTOR IN PROMOTING PRIVATE SECTOR DEVELOPMENT

At present, complaints are rampant about the failure of the public sector to provide a conducive environment for private sector development. The results of a private sector survey conducted by the World Bank on how private investors view the state is indeed revealing. Entrepreneurs were requested to provide their subjective evaluation on aspects of institutional framework in their countries consisting of security of property rights, predictability of rules and policies, problems with corruption and discretionary power in the bureaucracy, and disruptions due to change of government.

If the public sector is genuinely to support the private sector so that it can be an engine of growth, it has to take a number of measures. These include:

- **Creation of a stable macro-economic framework and predictable policies**

Ensuring a viable and sustainable macro-economic environment is a precondition for the growth of the financial system. Eliminating fiscal deficits and their financing through the central bank, and bringing down inflation to low, stable levels will significantly restore business confidence. Policy-makers have to recognise the primary role of entrepreneurs in the process of economic development and should engage the private sector in continuous dialogue in order to forge a closer partnership with it and avoid working at cross-purposes. Moreover, governments should make sure that a stable and predictable policy environment is in place. The turbulent policy environment obtaining in many developing countries has been sending confusing signals to entrepreneurs, making it difficult for them to make investment decisions.

- **Political stability**

No development can take place in the absence of a stable political environment. The political instability and civil strife rampant in some developing countries are not conducive to private sector development. Policies that are a prerequisite for the effective development of the private sector can only materialise in a situation of stable political environment.

- **A market-friendly policy stance and a civil service supportive of the private sector and capable of managing the regulatory system in a neutral manner**

As pointed out earlier, the effectiveness of the dominant state as an instrument of development has been seriously questioned and there is now a general agreement that the state should play a supportive and facilitative role.

It is necessary to have an effective civil service that is private sector-friendly and staffed with capable civil servants who can carry out their responsibilities efficiently. Having a productive civil service capable of supporting the efforts of the private sector in the development process requires well-motivated, adequately compensated and customer-oriented civil servants.

Privatisation is an important instrument for accelerating private sector development. Many developing countries have already embarked upon some sort of privatisation programmes. The pace of implementation is of course uneven but lately it has accelerated and the scope is widening. Hence, if the private sector is to play a lead role as the engine of growth, it has to be encouraged and supported by the government. Re-engineering the state becomes essential for national efficiency, transition to a market economy and the full development of the private sector. However, given the undeveloped and fragile nature of the private sector in the environment, it is expected that the state will continue to be involved in certain strategic areas of the economy.

- **Strengthening the financial sector**

A strong private sector cannot exist without a properly functioning financial system. The financial sector is expected to mobilise savings and efficiently channel to production and investment. In this regard, it is important that the banking infrastructure is improved and strengthened, the banking system restructured, capital markets deepened and micro-finance supported. Building an efficient financial sector for the mobilisation of domestic resources for the private investment requires "a sound payments and settlement system, reliable accounting and auditing procedures, more qualified and experienced personnel, and an effective supervisory system." (ADB, 160). As many banks remain distressed, measures have to be taken to recapitalise, restructure, privatise or liquidate. One of the serious constraints faced for the effective functioning of micro-and small enterprises is access to credit. Considering their number and potential in generating employment and alleviating of poverty, these enterprises need to be supported by facilitating their access to finance. In this respect, an African Development Bank Report remarks:

> Efforts should concentrate on upgrading informal financial arrangements, strengthening their links with formal institutions, and improving their links with formal institutions and improving the legal framework. ... Linkages between formal and informal institutions can be promoted by providing fiscal incentives, such as tax relief on the profits of formal financial institutions with informal linkages. Finally, there is a need to improve the legal environment through better definition and enforcement of property rights of MEs and SMEs. (ADB, 1997, p 161).

- **Establishing a foundation of law and improving the regulatory and legal framework**

The existence of the rule of law is considered a cornerstone of good governance. In the absence of laws that regulate social behaviour, societies can live under chaos. While this is true in a general sense, it becomes even more critical when viewed in the context of development. Where social order backed by institutions lacks, one cannot expect the market to function effectively. Property rights are central to the effective functioning of the market system. These property rights are central to the effective functioning of the market system. They provide the right signal that the market should operate in an atmosphere free from theft, violence and other acts of predation. Equally, for their effective functioning they require "protection from arbitrary government actions – ranging from unpredictable, ad hoc regulations and taxes to outright corruption – that disrupt business activity". Another important ingredient is reasonably fair and predictable judiciary laws relating to business contracts, property rights, collateral, debt recovery. A credible legal and judicial framework supportive of economic rights has to be introduced.

Much has been said about the legal and regulatory constraints to private sector development. As many countries move towards a market economy, it would be necessary to undertake reform measures that would facilitate the smooth transition and eventual proper functioning of the market system. Efficient regulatory systems have to be put in place.

- **Creating competition in the banking sector which crowds out the private sector**

Divestiture will facilitate intermediation between the banks, savers and investors and channel significant savings in informal channels into the formal banking system.

- **Dissemination of economic information**

Information is a critical input for promoting efficient resource allocation. In developing countries, it is the government that is in a position to generate and avail such information for producers and consumers alike who need it to protect their welfare and increase their efficiency.

- **Promotion of scientific and technological research**

Whether the promotion of technology is perceived as one to be imported or developed domestically, there is a need for government to be involved. The government should, therefore, create an atmosphere in which the promotion of technological and scientific research is made possible through grants, institutional support and linkages with international organisations.

- **Investing in basic social services and infrastructure**

Those countries that have performed well in their economies seem to have taken investment in social services and infrastructure very seriously. Evidence is also abundant that public investment in health, education and infrastructure yield high returns. With the exception of a few countries, investment has tended to follow non-productive sectors. There is now a consensus that the state should invest in health and education as well as in the development of transportation, communication and power systems. It is assumed, because of the high investment requirements and the slow yield that the private sector may not be attracted to these activities. It may, therefore, be necessary for the public sector to spearhead the initiative. But there is a possibility for the private sector also to be involved in partnership with government in such activities.

- **Support for small and medium-scale enterprises (SMEs)**

The recognition of SMEs as effective instruments of development has led governments to provide a central role to small and medium-scale enterprises in their development strategies. The case for genuine support to SMEs becomes apparent when one considers the significant contribution to the acceleration of economic development in Africa and Asia and when one takes into account their potential for development as manifested in their labour-intensive nature, income-generating possibilities, capital-saving capability, potential use of local resources and reliance on few imports, flexibility, innovativeness and strong linkages with the other sectors of the economy. There is a good case for governments to extend more genuine support to the sector.

However, in spite of their assumed importance as instruments of development, SMEs in many countries enjoy lukewarm support. They lack effective organisation and knowledge of modern management techniques. Organisations created to promote SMEs are not sufficiently prepared for the task and the interface with policy-makers leaves much to be desired.

- **Support for the informal sector**

Harnessing the entrepreneurial potential visible in the informal sector should be an integral component of private sector development. Many developing countries have yet genuinely to recognise the usefulness of this sector and institute supportive policies. Considering its sizeable role in the economy, governments have to find a mechanism to integrate the informal sector into the formal modern sector of the economy. Unfortunately, the informal sector continues to be harassed and intimidated by state authorities in some countries, in spite of the fact that it contributes as much as 20% to the GDP of many countries.

The informal sector generates employment opportunities for many. It provides a financial cushion and survival opportunities to the poor at a time of economic hardship. It provides training opportunities, thereby serving as a "breeding source" for entrepreneurs for SMEs. Moreover, it enables the entrepreneur to mobilise resources from grassroots institutions. By relying on family labour, the informal sector succeeds in holding costs down. Support for this sector can accelerate the graduation of entrepreneurs in the informal sector to SMEs.

- **Institutional and infrastructural needs for private sector development**

Certain critical institutions are required to support the development of the private sector. There is need for creating and enhancing institutional capacity in such areas as entrepreneurship development programmes, financial infrastructure, extension services and support institutions in Research and Development (R&D). Extension services could be extended through the establishment of industrial centres, industrial estates and business and technical incubators. Assistance in product design and improvement, assistance in the manufacturing of affordable machinery capable of using local raw materials and research capable of enhancing their local capacity to produce should be encouraged.

Industrial centres are needed to provide guidance and counselling on investment opportunities for modern small-scale industries, preparation and appraisal of pre-investment proposals and feasibility studies, preparation of market studies and area economic surveys, functional consultancy services in production management, accounting, marketing, extension services in installation and commissioning of new factory plants, repair and maintenance of equipment, in-plant technical assistance, etc.

Industrial estates make life easy for new entrepreneurs by providing ready-built factory sheds that can be let for a fee, thus enabling the entrepreneur to consolidate his/her limited resources to procure urgently needed equipment. In addition to the factory sheds, the industrial estates provide electricity, water, warehouses, central purchasing and central repairs facilities. Such facilities provided through industrial estates can go a long way towards reducing the overhead costs of entrepreneurs. This could be particularly useful in high-cost environments where the cost utilities and infrastructure can be prohibitive to the struggling, first-time entrepreneur. Technical incubators that provide a comprehensive range of common services including incubator space, enterprise counselling, shared secretariat, start-up financing and assistance with product development and marketing, could assist in enhancing the technical and managerial capacity of the entrepreneurs.

Research centres that provide information on the use of locally produced raw materials, the development of projects necessary for local raw material development and utilisation by the manufacturing sector, assisting with the development of appropriate technology for adoption by handicraft and small-scale industries, could provide useful services that would facilitate the operation of entrepreneurs.

Umbrella national organisations that provide one-stop services for entrepreneurs should be established. Likewise, there is a need to create institutional capacity for linkages with government to foster policy co-ordination through such mechanisms as Small Enterprise Development Councils, National Associations of SMEs, and dialogue fora between business associations, NGOs and governments.

- **Effective communication strategies**

There is, however, a need to strengthen the institutional mechanisms for consultation and communication between private and public sectors. More often than not, the poor dialogue can be attributed to ineffective communication between the two partners. Beyond communication, the challenge is to provide trained and capable operators and managers within the public sector who have the capacity and ability to engage the private sector in a meaningful dialogue on day-to-day issues as well as on strategic partnerships that need to be drawn up and negotiated, given the highly competitive global environment.

THE JUSTIFICATION AND NATURE OF THE LEGAL FRAMEWORK IN PARTNERSHIP PROMOTIONS

The operation of the public sector is largely the domain of the government and therefore the rules are the sole prerogative of the government in power. If the private sector has to be afforded an opportunity to play a meaningful role in the social-economic development of a nation then the rules of the game cannot remain the same as they were under the state-controlled system of nation-building. In accordance with modern phraseology, the "playing field must be levelled". This, in the final analysis, amounts to facilitating the involvement of the private sector in the development process. There is no doubt that any private sector involvement in the socio-economic development of any nation must be buttressed first and foremost by the confidence that the private sector has in the nation as a whole. Three key areas that enhance confidence in the nation and its institutions are: democratic rule; good governance; and the rule of law.

- **Democratic rule**

A democratic system of government ensures that the government in power is accountable to the people and to the laws of the nation. Ultimately, the people exercise the power to make and un-make a government. The notion of checks and balances through the separation of powers provides the backbone for transparency and accountability and therefore keeps the government in power under constant check. There must be a meaningful role played by the opposition as well as the press. The net result is that there is rule of law, transparency and accountability. It is imperative for a democratic institution to be in place if the public and private partnership is to be viable. Where the government exercises absolute power, there is the tendency to abuse political and economic power, resulting in the absence of transparency and accountability.

- **Good governance**

Democratic government does not necessarily lead to good governance. At best it provides the basis for it. The ultimate aim of the public/private sector partnership is to achieve an optimum level of development; and this can best be enhanced under a system of good governance. It has been noted that "[G]ood governance is vital for economic development because it complements sound rules and economic policies" (Kahkonen et al 1997: 47). Governance has been defined by the United Nations Development Programme as "the exercise of political, economic and administrative authority in the management of a country's affairs at all levels. Governance comprises the complex mechanisms, processes and institutions through which citizens and groups articulate their interests, mediate their differences and exercise their legal rights and obligations" (UNDP 1997a: iv). This is consistent with the World Bank definition "to denote the use of political authority and exercise of control in a society in relation to the management of its resources for social and economic development" (OECD) 1995: 14). The legitimacy and transparent nature of the exercise of the governance will determine whether it is good or not.

Through the practice of good governance, the opposition is able to articulate its views and the citizenry have the freedom to exercise the rights and opportunities necessary for participatory democracy. The transparent nature of the formulation and implementation of policies instils confidence in the population and removes any inhibition that militates against participation in the development of the nation. Civil society and the press operate freely without any inhibitions. The cumulative effect is that all these impact positively on every aspect of the nation and private sector confidence is equally enhanced.

- **The Rule of Law**

A major factor that has the potential to instil both public and private sector confidence in a country's institutions is the operation of the rule of law. "The rule of law is ... an essential factor for the effective functioning of the society and the economy" (OECD 1995: 14). If the rule of law is respected in a country, the popular notion of separation of powers is put into practice and "a predictable legal environment, with an objective, reliable and independent judiciary" (OECD ibid), will be in operation. The rule of law ensures that all institutions of the nation are subjected to the laws of the country, strict code of conduct, accountability and transparent procedures. The most essential element here, which is the cornerstone for allaying the fears of the private sector, is the independence of the judiciary. If the independence of the judiciary is guaranteed, the community as a whole lives under the realisation that, in the event of a dispute or wrongful action emanating from whichever quarter, there will be a recourse for redress. The partnership will be meaningless and private participation will not be forthcoming if the tendency is for infringements to be ignored. No person or an organisation in the private sector will be willing to pour capital into a system where the judiciary cannot be expected to provide credible remedy when rights are infringed. If the laws of the country are disregarded or flouted with impunity, especially by those in authority, it creates a state of uncertainty and near anarchy.

The rule of law is not an abstract entity. It calls for a nation to have clearly defined laws, starting particularly with the constitution which defines the powers of government and the elimination of any form of abuse of power. For it to be effective and acceptable it demands "the creation of honest law enforcement agencies that effectively carry out court decisions, and a court administration that ensures that cases are dealt with expeditiously (OECD

1995:15). Where there are "inefficiencies in the legal system, such as lack of predictability, delays in handling court cases and lack of enforcement of law decisions, increase business costs, discourage investors and obstruct development" (ibid).

CREATING THE RIGHT LEGAL ENVIRONMENT

As was pointed out earlier, without a predictable legal environment, many investors are reluctant to invest in a country. Where the whole legal machinery seems to have broken down and there is no law and order, the tendency for foreign investors to shy away from the economy increases. South Africa offers the best example as many foreign investors have expressed their reluctance to invest in the country, because of the high level of the crime rate. In the Sunday Times (13 September, 1998) it was reported that 74% of the highly skilled South Africans were prepared to emigrate and they cited the crime rate as the primary reason. The report states: "The major reason for considering leaving is crime, according to 62 per cent of respondents" (p 5). In order to control the trend, law enforcement should be strengthened.

If one were to identify the most serious flaw in the post-independence era of many developing countries, any objective analyst should have no hesitation in identifying lack of accountability and indiscipline resulting from the non-implementation and non-enforcement of laws and decisions as the major cause. It is one thing to have laws on the statue books, and another to implement decisions and the laws. When the laws are there for the sake of being there, they become a scarecrow to the population. This has been the trend in many countries since independence. The developmental failures can be attributed directly to this phenomenon. Tax evasion, non-payment of customs and exercise duties, corruption, fraudulent business transactions, lack of confidence in the security forces and the judiciary are all interlinked with the popular notion that there is a breakdown of law and order. The crucial question that arises is whether most of the developing countries have the capacity to create a predictable legal environment in which investor confidence can be assured so as to enhance the public and private partnership relationship for the development of the countries. Any objective assessment of the situation reveals that the story is the same in most capitals around the continent.

As has been stressed earlier, the major hindrance to private sector participation, particularly the foreign investor, in the development of some countries is the security situation in most of the developing countries. Furthermore, the breakdown of law and order and the lack of public confidence in the whole machinery of the administration of justice also militate against investor confidence. For instance corruption, which is seen as a major contributory factor to under-development in many third world countries ("corruption restricts investment and holds back economic growth"), thrives in an environment where one can cheat and get away with it.

Under those circumstances, it is essential that some innovative and radical steps be put forward for consideration. Principal among these is the need for the public and private sectors to team up to ensure that "a predictable legal environment" is created. It is also essential to identify key areas where collaboration with the private sector will impact positively on the laws governing the business arena as a whole.

CONCLUSION

The concept of public and private sector partnership, while not new, has been in existence in many countries in one form or another. Outsourcing arrangements for example, where a public authority retains ownership or policy control of a function but contracts with a private operator to discharge it. While they may lack the precise legal characteristics of formal partnerships under commercial law regimes, contracting arrangements of this sort certainly mix public and private interests and endeavours.

Another example of public and private sector partnership is a situation in which a government pays substantial subsidies to private companies to get them to do things the government does not want to do itself, such as the development of aviation services in Australia's sparsely populated outback, and defence production in the United States, where large private firms produce under contract to service government orders and whose very existence often depends on those contracts. These kinds of partnership will exist in many Commonwealth countries in one form or another but may need to be strengthened where they do exist or where the private sector is insignificant, such as in small island states in the Caribbean and the South Pacific.

The role of the state, therefore, is to play a key role in the provision of public goods and services and to create and sustain an environment that fosters strong and equitable development. Governments establish the rules that make markets work efficiently and also correct market failures. In order to play such a role, the state needs revenue and human resources as well as systems that are responsible for revenue collection and produce public goods and services. This, in turn, requires proper systems and procedures of accountability, adequate and reliable information, and efficiency in resource management and the delivery of public service. Public/private sector interface is currently being strengthened and pursued by many developing countries in the ways described above.

From observation and analysis of this interface, it appears that, in future, partnership will be driven more vigorously by global inter-dependence, the communication or information technology revolution and, more importantly, the expectation of the public to be involved in the decisions of government. The pressures for democracy are likely to become more immediate and direct as a result of globalisation. Public and private sector partnership is likely to be intensified as one of the ways of solving the problems of poverty, and meeting the need for better education, health, housing and basic needs. The requirement for a joint solution is based on the assumption that the public sector alone can no longer cope with the demands for improvement, not only in delivery but also in the quality of service to the public.

The shift in paradigm requiring the state to abandon its traditional role seems to have been pushed too far at times. Even though its involvement in the productive sector of the economy may have raised doubts about its effectiveness in that area, there are still a number of important roles it has to play in support of development. The choice should not be reduced to one between state and market, but rather between different mixes of state and market.

Indeed it could be argued that in the context of good governance, the challenge is for a country to mobilise its resources to optimise the mix of public and private partnerships for the greater good. Performance benchmarks could then be developed to measure over time how a given country managed its development programme on the basis of a renewed public service and a productive private sector for mutual benefit and, ultimately, for the development of the country.

At a time when the private sector is being required to assume a significant role in development, the public sector has to ensure that the assumption of such a responsibility is facilitated. The public sector can, in the framework of its new role, promote, strengthen and nurture the private sector. The areas of collaboration identified in this publication could be a starting point. With the fast-changing global environment, which does not seem to be promising for many countries, at least in the short run, the public and private sectors have to join hands and map out a common strategy so as to minimise the impact of being marginalised in the global economy. Contrary to past thinking when the private and public sectors viewed one another as adversaries, today there is a recognition that their roles are complementary and that they should work in co-operation and partnership.

REFERENCES

African Development Bank, 1997, Fostering Private Sector Development in Africa, Oxford University Press.

Klitgaard, R. 1994. Institutional reform and the challenge facing South Africa. University of Natal. Report funded under IRIS agreement with K. Klitgaard.

Mukandala, R. 1998. "Post-Privatisation Issues", in Asmelash Beyene (ed), Privatization in Africa: Trends and Lessons, DPMF Bulletin.

The World Bank 1997. The State in a Changing World. Oxford University Press.

Commonwealth Currents, 2/97. London, England.

PUBLIC AND PRIVATE SECTOR VALUES
IN PARTNERSHIP STRENGTHENING

INTRODUCTION

The debate on the role of values both within the public and private sectors and between the public and the individual person, has always aimed at examining the possible ways of improving the delivery of service to the people. It has, therefore, been used as an instrument either for change or for continuity of dealing with issues and concerns. The conflicts between the two sets of values, depending on how they are used in the management process, can either have a negative or positive impact on the delivery of service. This can occur in situations that can generate or stagnate change. However, the symbiosis of the two sets of values might produce co-operation and collaboration, which are necessary in managing the development process and forging partnership.

Defining a concept is always a problem in the sense that it brings different meanings to different people. In this regard, we shall attempt to define values and would argue that what is more important is not necessarily the definition but its impact on the public and private sector partnership.

Dewar has defined values as "a framework of beliefs and convictions that motivate behaviour and provide guidance for making choices among possible courses of action".[1] Sometimes people confuse values with ethics. While they appear to convey the same meaning, ethics are really a set of principles that guide behaviour in the action process. Ethics may not be written but assumed, based on the past practices and interests of the stakeholders. In general, such ethics are written for the purposes of training, learning the principles of the occupation and guiding behaviour partners in partnership development.

Some ethics and values are emphasised more in the public sector than in the private sector. Neutrality, for example, might be expected more of a public servant than it is of the private sector employee. This may be so because of the type of service, the status of the client and what is expected from the customer. In the private sector it may depend on what business the customer is likely to bring to the organisation directly.

In the past and within the civil service, values such as neutrality, loyalty, obedience, continuity etc. were the golden symbols upon which promotion and rewards were based. This contrasts markedly with some of the virtues in the private sector where assertiveness, aggressiveness in marketing product, pro-activity and profit motive may be the guidelines for the advancement of the employee in the organisation.

These values and ethics are expected to assist employees in visualising the ideal outcomes and help to establish the goals and objectives of the organisation. In addition, they contribute towards the motivation of workers in the promotion of the organisation's goals. While the values help workers to defuse their roles in the organisation, they also serve as standards against which progress can be measured, giving rise to stability in times of crisis.

The experience within the public service has shown that values, once they have been acquired, tend to be instinctive, valid and finally become internalised by becoming a part of a behavioural pattern without questioning the rationale and value of such behaviour.

The unanimity and magnanimity of public service values pose the question of their relevance in the private sector that may have a different philosophy and management practices. Most countries in the Commonwealth are currently emphasising the important role of private enterprise as an economic philosophy. The question that can be posed is what kind of values does the public service need to develop in order to deliver its services to a society that has accepted a new or modified *modus operandi* and/or a revised programme based on a new and well-articulated ethos. Alternatively, can the public service deliver its service under a different form?

In essence, values and ethics are supposed to guide behaviour at work and, more importantly, guide the manner in which public or private sector services are delivered. This also includes the manner in which customers are treated at the point of receiving a service.

PUBLIC ADMINISTRATION AND PUBLIC MANAGEMENT

There are at least two schools of thought on the interpretation of the two concepts, namely, Public Administration and Public Management. One school assumes that public administration is based on the need to maintain stability, law and order, continuity and loyalty. Furthermore, it is guided by such values as neutrality, integrity, accountability etc. Under the civil service code, in some countries, the violation of the values of neutrality and integrity is often a punishable offence.

One of the violations is regarded as bringing the integrity of the civil service into "disrepute". The interpretation of "disrepute" is often left to the administrator or supervisor or manager.

The other school of thought assumes that public management is different from public administration. According to this school of thought, public management is based on such values as efficiency, effectiveness, responsiveness to the market and consumers and assertiveness. In general, administration values are applicable to the pubic sector while management is regarded as forming the main ethos within the private sector or business enterprise.

Some practitioners would argue that the transfer of the civil service from the colonial government to the nationalist self-rule was based on the public administration paradigm which aimed at continuity, reference to precedents and unquestionable obedience. New colonialism has therefore been maintained and supported by the values found in public administration. On the contrary, capitalism has been based on the profit motive which outweighs all other considerations. Business people are often viewed as aggressive, proactive, etc. in the interests of making business flourish. Businessmen are often associated with dynamism, orientation to change and progress towards identified objectives, while administration is closely associated with the resistance to change, emphasis on continuity and the top-down approach to decision-making.

Ideologically, the debate on these two paradigms (administration and management) appears to be linked to neo-colonialism and private enterprise respectively. Whichever way the two paradigms are viewed, they are perceived by practitioners as being the focus of conducting government (public) business and private enterprise respectively.

There is a general assumption that the manner in which service is delivered to a client or customer depends upon the paradigm being used. The values of efficiency and effectiveness, time-keeping and immediate response to the customer are often associated with the private sector. The contrary is also alleged to be true, that is, public service is associated with inefficiency, poor time-keeping and non-responsiveness to the client in the delivery of service. Because of these arguments, public servants are associated with insensitivity and ineffectiveness. These views erroneously influence the minds of the people and have in some ways confirmed the view that civil servants are neither hard-working nor concerned about their clients' needs. One of the major differences between these two paradigms is based on ownership of the organisation. The ownership principle is based on the premise that one would want to see that "what belongs to him" succeeds as one depends on the business enterprise for one's livelihood. This is contrary to the behaviour of an employee of an enterprise that is publicly owned. However, there is no scientific evidence that a person is more likely to be efficient if he or she owns the enterprise. The students of public administration and public management should address this problem in the era of technological change or the restructuring of the civil service. In other words, is the question of ownership a factor in the reform of the public service?

This question arises out of some of the recommendations given to public services such as privatisation, forming co-operatives, and commercialisation which all have an element of ownership. Indirectly, therefore, private enterprise is used as a means of decontrolling public ownership thereby giving the power to owners of enterprises. The question that can be asked is whether this is a mistaken belief or a reality. This trend should be grasped by the leaders of the reform process in the public service.

THE IMPLICATIONS FOR REFORM

The public services of most countries are under pressure to change. Change is caused by both external and internal factors. Many developing countries are confronted by turbulent international markets, uncertain flows of aid and other external financing, as well as political instability.[2] The pressures to privatise some parts of the public enterprise also lead to domestic changes being made. Within the countries themselves, pressures to change are brought about by rising unemployment, high interest rates, devaluation and the degeneration of health, education, housing, environment and other social services. These pressures have resulted in the inevitable development of new thinking and perception of the need for better planning and forecasting of future opportunities and constraints. Many countries have realised that their capacity to deal with these problems is limited. They have also realised that short-term crisis management is inadequate for what is generally seen as a long-term process of solving the problems. They have equally realised that they need to put in place a system that can facilitate and anticipate changes, and manage uncertainty and complexity.

Concomitant with pressures to change, thought processes and policies are also pressures to change management systems that no longer serve the interests of the consumers. The pressures to change are taking place simultaneously at four levels: first, the philosophy that guides action has to change. It can no longer give answers to the problems identified. The philosophy can no longer be managed in a manner that can deliver the expected results. The second level is the changing social environment. The environment is no longer conducive to maintaining the *status quo*. It is also changing itself since it is not static. The environment consists of the people, pressure groups, non-governmental organisations and international interest groups. Thirdly, the consumers of service are now highly politicised. They are demanding not only better and more service but also a better quality of service. The changes and demands by consumers are consistent with the dynamic changes taking place in society. This appears more critical in countries that are moving from a dictatorship or one-party state to a democratic and multi-party state. Fourthly, the management system and the values under which it operates are facing severe pressure to change. The methods of operation and the structures of departments would need to respond to the overall changes taking place in society. It also becomes clear that public service values such as anonymity, confidentiality, or secrecy can no longer serve a new society that is open and consensus-building. The "routinisation" associated with public bureaucracy may no longer be appropriate for a dynamic society. The notion of permanence at work as in the public service is no longer compatible with the ideas of contract and setting targets. The evaluation of performance no longer entirely focuses on compliance, obedience, respect or some personal characteristics but on achieving the set goals efficiently and effectively.

Demands are also being made to change the management procedures in financial matters, information management systems, accountability procedures and policy formulation and implementation.

The conflicting values can clearly be seen in at least four management systems:

- The improvement of performance management system is now related to newly formed labour laws, for example, negotiations on salaries and conditions of service. Further, they are based on new principles in the areas of recruitment, promotion and training. In some countries, the confidential reports have been replaced by an open system in which the supervisor and supervisee discuss problem areas of performance. Secrecy no longer surrounds performance appraisals.

- The restructuring of ministries has meant that there are fewer chains of command, the size of the service is reduced, channels of communication are reduced and organisations are dynamic and must achieve the set goals and objectives. Restructuring also assumes role changes and goal direction, each requiring a set of values and principles of operations. Restructuring allows the organisation to get rid of old staff who are resistant to change and consequently allow new blood, which has a high degree of absorptive capacity in a changing organisation with changing goals and dynamic environment.

- The management of human and financial resources has assumed different dimensions with new strategies in place. The new thinking and practices in financial management now include such topical issues as the reporting of both financial and non-financial information, managing core budget processes, accrual accounting performance measures and appropriation. The performances of chief executives and permanent secretaries are now amenable to public scrutiny.[3] The values of secrecy and compliance will be at odds with the business culture that is adopted following restructuring of the organisation.

- Decentralised decision-making makes it possible for services to be delivered immediately rather than wait for a decision from headquarters. Decentralisation may include devolution of powers, discussion between sectoral and functional roles, which are meant to be responsive to the needs of the clients or consumers of policy. The values of an open system are likely to be at odds with the values of a closed system and this has negative implications for the human resources that manage the organisation.

POLICY DECISIONS

A public service that has been used to formulating policy decisions in secrecy, e.g. the Official Secrets Acts, would find it extremely difficult to open up, consult and collaborate with other stakeholders in the process. The difficulty arises out of the inherent conflicts and contradictions between the values of secrecy and openness. In the last few years, in many of the public services, a practice of consultation and consensus-building between and among policy-makers has developed. The implementation and evaluation of such policy decisions would be equally meaningful and effective if there were sufficient consultation and co-operation. When the policy is being implemented, people would be aware of the issues and not be taken by surprise, as they are in situations where decisions are made secretly. In general, it has been found that where people are involved there is less resistance to change or the implementation of a policy decision. Consensus-building is therefore much easier when the appropriate steps have been followed than when people are told to implement decisions which have been made without their involvement.[4] From experience, it is possible to identify critical factors in decision-making processes. These factors are political commitment, ownership of change, leadership by example, and training for human resources. Training is an important variable in the decision-making process, to the extent that it enables people to change their behavioural patterns and attitudes to reforms. It is often the case that people in decision-making positions are expected to change from, for example, secrecy to openness. In such cases, there is always a possibility of either unconscious resistance or deliberate attempts to prevent changes taking place. Such examples are particularly common in the restructuring of the pubic service. A civil servant for example, who was on fixed or permanent establishment is unlikely to co-operate in the proposed changes for a contract system which may be a threat to him or her. This is made worse by a civil servant who is about to retire on account of advanced age. In this regard, it is always important to identify all possible areas of potential resistance before any changes are introduced. The value would be at variance with the temporary conditions of employment such as a contract system.

In one country, permanent secretaries rejected a contract system for them in the restructuring exercise. This meant that they took their own interests into account and not those of the organisation that was being reformed. One other dimension of resistance to a contract system is related to the quality and efficiency of staff themselves. Hard-working and entrepreneurial civil servants are more likely to take up early retirement or redundancy packages than the incompetent, lazy and inactive public servants. One of the reasons is that the assertive public servant can get a job anywhere while the dead wood or lazy civil servants are threatened by such packages because they know that they would not be able to make it in a competitive society. This is aggravated by factors associated with key competence areas, which are mainly based on skills, knowledge, technology and capital.

RESULTS

Within the current restructuring of the public services of many of the Commonwealth countries, there is an assumption, backed up by a few examples, that private sector values, practices, methods and procedures of work should be applied to the public sector if it is to be efficient and responsive to the needs of the consumers. The government in this regard should concentrate on what it can do with its skills and not be involved in areas in which it is not competent and does not have the requisite skills, technology and human resources. According to this argument, the state should hand over all those functions where private enterprise principles operate to the private sector, which has expertise in the area.

There is a school of thought that assumes that there is no conflict between the values of the public sector and those found in the private sector. The difference has been in the degree and intensity of the use of such values as assertiveness, neutrality etc. In other words, one can apply neutrality and confidentiality in the private sector just as much as in the public sector. The difference here is the nature and type of social environment in which the principles are applied. While the environments (public and private sectors) are not contradictory and sometimes target the same clientele, the approaches to business may be the same. The setting up of targets and the openness of governance peculiar to the private sector can also be applied to the public sector, perhaps with better results.

It is therefore argued that some of the values and approaches used in the private sector can equally be applied to the public sector, taking into account the uniqueness and concrete conditions existing in the public sector. The successful application of values and approaches depends on the skills, knowledge and resources available. At the end of the day, it is the person who is delivering the service, the manner in which he/she does it and the political commitment and will he/she is given by the management that is at the root of the argument. For this reason, the advocates of this premise would argue that it is possible to place a permanent secretary in an executive position in the private sector. The opposite can also be true, that is, taking the chief executive of a private enterprise and placing him/her in the position of a permanent secretary in a comparable and compatible ministry. Such an inter-change of personalities at a high level will enrich the experiences of both people because of their exposure to different environments and organisational systems.

The adoption of private enterprise values by the public sector is likely to have varying results on the organisations, the staff, the social environments and the clients or consumers of public policy. In general, the following are a few of the possible key result areas:

- *Stress of managers*

Any change is likely to cause anxiety, uncertainty and stress for those who are managing change and this will inevitably and indirectly affect the clients or the masses. Stress may also come about because there is no precedent of dealing with issues. The old order has been changed and a whole new parameter for change is being worked out.

The civil service in particular has been in the habit of using the "accounting officer's instructions" or "Treasury instructions" to solve problems. The changes taking place may have no reference to the past or to the instructions, and further, there is no textbook. In these circumstances, strategic management becomes appropriate as an instrument of responding to change. The success of handling stress will also depend on the skills, attitude, experience and tolerance of the manager. The manager can also enrich his knowledge of handling crisis by attending some courses on stress management that may be offered by the local management institute. In management, stress can be caused by at least two factors and these are change and role strain. "Role strain can be caused by not being involved in decision making, having inadequate managerial support, having to cope with technological or other changes, having to maintain standards of performance even under difficult circumstances, having responsibility for people who are uncooperative."[5]

- *Organisational and structural change*

Change has also a direct impact on the organisation itself. The objectives, procedures, technology, methods of recruitment, training and discipline may change. Such change has an impact on middle managers who have to ensure that the right procedures are implemented. Staff may be expected to acquire new skills and tasks or they may be re-graded and transferred to other departments. The organisation may be restructured, which will have consequences on the reduction of the size of the civil service, the abolition of posts and levels of management, and the expectations on new and appropriate academic qualifications. Within the public service we have heard such concepts as de-layering, decentralisation, deregulation and democratisation processes, each of which has implied changes and values and principles for reform. Change itself might mean that new methods and procedures have to be learnt and that it might affect the self-esteem of some managers. A combination of all these factors can affect the performance of both the organisation and the individual.

- *Attitudinal change*

When assumptions underlying value systems change, managers and staff are likely to respond in many different ways. Apart from uncertainty, staff can resist change unconsciously or may deny that change exists. Such denial of change may affect perception of work and performance of the individual. Denial may lead to disregarding the new rules and substituting them with the old ones with which staff may be familiar. Openness is one of the virtues that will be difficult to internalise for a closed system. The democratisation process has often been hindered by the previous unquestionable closed system. This is fairly common in organisations that may change at the top without the involvement of the middle and line managerial levels.

- *Efficiency and effectiveness*

In most departments and public enterprises where some of the values have been applied there has been a noticeable improvement in efficiency. Goods and services have been delivered on time with limited costs. In some cases, expenditures have been reduced while, at the same time, clients have been satisfied with the service. Equally, in other circumstances the quality of service has improved and objectives have been achieved at less cost. The road is not always smooth as there can be conflicts with existing and predominant values. The critical factor in the application of these value systems is the choice of the relevant values. The manager and his or her team must always diagnose their organisation and select the right type of solution based on certain acceptable values.

- *Strategic plans*

Many departments have been forced by the situation to develop strategic plans for their organisations. Such plans have been developed through and with the co-operation of line and front managers and their staff. There has been an element of ownership of strategic plans. The strategic plans have been useful in as far as the staff could see how the resources were utilised, the financial management methods used, and above all the direction that the department was taking within its limited means and constraints. The advantage of such plans has been that they are based on consensus-building, team-work, and support given to staff who may be lost in the organisation.

Strategic plans have also clearly stated the goals of the department and have articulated the values upon which their methods of operations are based. Customer care, integrity, loyalty, team spirit and open management style are examples of values that have been successfully implemented in many government departments, public enterprises and local authorities and even non-government organisations. The question that arises out of the absorption of these value assumptions by the public sector is to what extent and with what resources they can be implemented in an organisation. Below we try to answer these and many other questions and issues concerning the management of change.

AGENDA FOR BRINGING ABOUT CHANGE

When policy decisions are made at the highest level, the low-level managerial cadres are not involved, although they are supposed to implement the decisions. The values of frontline managers are critical to any structural or incremental change that is proposed. From experience of other countries, it would appear that the most successful changes have occurred when the following programmes of action are employed:

- A clearly formulated strategic plan that states the benefits to be achieved, the rationale for changes and the costs involved. The plan should be understood and accepted by the staff of the organisation. The modalities of executing the functions and values adopted should be clearly stated.

- The support from the highest level (political or administrative) is crucial to the success of the changes. It is important that senior managers are clearly accountable so that people can see how expenditure is being controlled and how financial resources are secured. A project management approach might be necessary since this involves both the users and line managers.

- The plan must show an element of ownership by the users. Services are better delivered when people know that they own the project. Customer care is likely to be reflected more easily when the users know that they participated in the formulation of the plan.

- When the purpose of change has been agreed, the chief executive should design the implementation stages in such a way that there is compatibility with the existing system, procedures, cultures and traditions. Ensuring maximum compatibility creates a better basis for implementation.

- The leadership should be exemplary. He or she should be seen to practise the values that the organisation wishes to adopt. Consequently, the managerial behaviour must change too. If, for example, there is need to reduce public expenditure, the head of state or minister should also behave in a manner consistent with the policy. The posts for example, which were created for the purposes of prestige, should be abolished in times of crisis in which public expenditure is expected to be reduced.

- All the value systems and new organisational procedures adopted can be strengthened by training and appropriate support systems. Training should be appropriate to managerial levels and line management staff training helps people to change their attitudes and behavioural patterns.

INTERACTION OF EMERGING ISSUES

The debate on public and private sector values has centred on the potential of applying the private sector ethos to the public sector. The values that enable a business enterprise to succeed are considered appropriate to the public service, especially in the context of structural or incremental changes that are currently in place or about to be implemented. It is assumed that the ideas of competition and choice, which appear to have engineered success of delivery of service in the private sector, can be applied with success in the public sector. Competition and choice have inbuilt values which enable the deliverers of service to become more customer-oriented, based on the need to satisfy their demands. It is also assumed that competition and choice result in efficiency, customer care, effectiveness, responsiveness and continuity of service. In essence, it is the adaptability to change and the responsiveness to market forces that will engender appropriate value systems. The change of value systems is not an easy one as there will be some elements of resistance to change, particularly by those who are likely to lose when changes occur. Within the civil service, resistance to change can be expressed through low morale, uncertainty about the future, poor performance, job security, high stress etc. The down-sizing of the civil service has, in some instances, been associated with loss of jobs, lack of job opportunities, concerns about new job expectations and limited investment in training for job opportunities. Unfortunately, the public sector has been putting a lot of emphasis on the restructuring of organisations and little on intensifying training or change of value systems. Restructuring has therefore, in some areas, resulted in undermining the old public service values of loyalty, permanence, job security, obedience, intelligence, continuity and impartiality.

The interchangeability of the value system has led some decision-makers to believe that it is possible for chief executives in the private sector to be brought into government as permanent secretaries and vice versa. Consequently, some governments are now advertising the posts of permanent secretaries to allow more competition and increase the choice of candidates. In some cases, methods of attachments or secondment to public sector posts and vice versa have been considered, and the result has not yet been fully investigated. In all these reforms, the leadership should be firmly committed and convinced that changes will be effective if implemented.

One of the major results of the interchangeability of values is that a new culture, a new way of conducting public business, a new thought process and a new structure without precedents have been born. A combination of all these new approaches and values will produce a modified or a reformed management structure capable of sustaining changes. It will also form the basis upon which good governance is measured and partnership built. Another result is that a new relationship, with different sets of parameters, between the public and private sectors, is reviewed and reconstructed. The reconstruction of this social reality reduces the animosity, jealousy and envy that are often found between the private and public sectors. The building of these bridges between the two sectors is made possible by the demands of the changing social environment, which aims to reduce the "them and us" situation that is still predominant in many countries.

The new mode of operation and partnership which underpin good governance can constitute a different management paradigm with a capacity to absorb change processes based on the interchangeability of value systems and the need to respond effectively to the needs of society.

The third result is that there appears to be efficiency, effectiveness, good customer care, good governance, productivity and improvement in service delivery by the public sector when the new and emerging management paradigm is being used. To the extent that some success has been scored in the utilisation of the paradigm, lessons can be drawn from specific countries that implemented new procedures based on the new value system.

The new public management paradigm is associated with a new organisational culture for example, setting standards, value for money, courtesy and helpfulness, information and openness.[6] Such values have brought to the fore the need for better methods of managing the public sector such as commercialisation, contracting out and privatisation. Further, there has been greater delegation of responsibilities to lower levels of management or to public enterprises. The restructuring of departments has led to the identification of better methods of managing human and financial resources. Human resources are now rewarded for their productivity and performance and the value system has had to change to suit the new environment with its new expectations and standards.

PUBLIC/PRIVATE SECTOR PARTNERSHIP

The interchangeability of the value system between the public and private sectors can contribute to the development of the culture of organisation. The culture of organisation (public and private) refers to the sentiments, behaviours, deeply held values, routines and accepted ways of doing things that become part of the fabric of the organisation. It is assumed that the culture of any organisation significantly influences and shapes the staff's and the management's ways of doing and thinking about the challenges and issues facing the organisation.[7]

Out of this public/private sector organisational culture emerge attitudinal, value and organisational factors of culture and these are:

▪ Attitudinal factors are termed promoting a performance culture, work satisfaction, discipline, specialist orientation and independence. The performance culture refers to the internal systems and controls that are considered helpful and supportive and curb wastage in the use of resources. Work satisfaction is considered to emerge from having a role which challenges and stimulates the incumbent as well as providing the opportunity to utilise skills and abilities as appropriate, whereas discipline in the pursuit of task and initiatives is an important element of working in a senior position.

▪ Value factors comprise work practices, service-oriented values, professionalism and conduct values, rights and duties values and workplace democracy values.

The work practices relate to those behaviours and orientations that are identified as supportive of high levels of individual contribution and performance. The service-oriented values highlight the need for respect of others, for supportive leadership and efficiency and effectiveness in the organisation in order to provide innovative and quality services to clients and value to the community. Characteristics of organisational and community values are social justice, morale of employees and organisational reputation. The rights and duties values highlight the importance of being held accountable for the discharge of responsibilities in the public office. The workplace values emphasise respect and caring for people as well as the involvement of others in the dialogue and decision-making process concerning work-related issues.

- Organisational performance factors comprise service delivery and interfacing across the structure. The service delivery effectiveness refers to the degree to which staff and management focus on key client groups and entertain a high level quality of discourse on to how to respond to clients' requirements. Equally, management's ability to deliver goods and services on time, be more responsive to meeting new initiatives and evolve a better thought-through strategic policy for the future, are considered as equally important elements for the effectiveness of service delivery. The performance of people in the organisation relates to issues of trust, morale, quality of internal relationships and a reduction in the number of inaccurate and unrealistic commitments being made to clients. Improvement in these areas is considered to stimulate overall better performance.

Strategic direction refers to the quality of thinking displayed by senior management as to how current changes generally, and changes in community requirements and demands specifically, are likely to affect the current running of the organisation. Such clarity of understanding needs to be equally applied to the issues affecting long-term strategy and how that will impact on the separate departments within the organisation.

Interfacing across the structure relates to examining the quality of relationship between central office and regional offices, divisions and subsidiaries themselves.[8]

These attitudinal, value, organisational and information technology factors are practised in different forms in both the public and private sectors. They contribute not only to the improvement in the management of the organisation but also impact directly on the effective and efficient delivery of services, whether by the public or private sector organisations.

The potential interchangeability of culture can be illustrated by the changes that are currently under consideration for the British civil service, particularly at the top managerial level of permanent secretary. The Times (24 August 99) of London, in a front-page article, reported that the Prime Minister was planning to hold top civil servants accountable for the delivery of Labour's manifesto promises.[9] The plan of the meeting was based on the slow speed in which Whitehall was putting policy into action and getting results. Earlier, the Prime Minister had shown his exasperation, saying he bore "scars on my back" after two years of trying to secure change in the public sector and in public services.[10] The move for change was part of an effort to transform the culture in Whitehall and make it more businesslike and responsive to change in order to improve the delivery of services to the public. The changes that were contemplated for implementation in the public service were for example, placing permanent secretaries on short-term contracts, performance agreements tied to the spending levels set for each department and ensuring that, by the end of the year, they have identified individuals with creative ideas and rewarded them with pay or promotion. The heads of department were, in addition, to be involved in modernising public services and, in particular, to ensure that many more women and ethnic minority staff got top jobs.

As a result of these pressures from the Prime Minister, Sir Richard Wilson, the Cabinet Secretary was expected to reach an agreement with his colleagues on measures to recruit fresh talent, reward risk-takers and innovators and break down the stuffy image of the civil service. Such initiatives were also expected to include amongst other issues, the opening up of top jobs to competition both from within the public service and from the private sector and wider public, and the rewarding of financial incentives to civil servants at all levels who come up with innovative and even risky ideas.

All these attempts to modernise the civil service through inculcating some of the values in the private sector constitute ways and means of strengthening the public and private sector partnership. These attempts, while not new processes or arrangements in management, have a potential to revolutionalise old ways of doing things and to provide a very positive leap into the future.

The consequences of the interaction of issues, demands, expectations and needs within the public/private sector delivery of service can be summarised under four categories:

- The public, like the private sector, is expected to be user-friendly as well as employee-friendly. According to this view, public sector is expected to encourage its public servants and anyone else who interacts with the public to treat the public as a customer very much as it is assumed they would be treated when in contact with the private sector.

- The public sector is supposed to become more friendly to its own employees, especially employees at the bottom of the organisational hierarchies. Governments are being driven to become less hierarchical, with the lower echelons of public organisations being empowered to make more decisions on their own. This empowerment reflects the reality that most decisions that are important to average citizens (consumers) are made at the lowest echelons of a bureaucracy. It also reflects a management style intended to give a great deal of latitude and responsibility to lower level workers within the context of a strong corporate culture that guides their actions.

- In addition to the above, the public sector is expected to emphasise the importance of quality in public programmes. Total quality management (TQM) has become common practice in much of the private sector and is becoming more common in the public sector. The concept (TQM) is that just as the public employees are being empowered to make more decisions, they should be involved in generating ideas about improving the services rendered to the public. Quality in this view becomes a shared concern for the entire organisation.

- Another important issue is the enhancement of participation in government. This is especially true for clients of public organisations but consultation and control – or at least influence – over policies is an increasingly important feature of policy in a number of countries. This style of decision-making may enhance the legitimacy of decisions once they are made.[11]

The four categories of consequences outlined above together constitute a series of attempts by the state to pursue a format for governance that will be at once efficient, effective and democratic. The fundamental direction, however, has been to make a government function more like the private sector in some respects. This tendency is captured well in the phrases "new public management, or reinvention or re-engineering etc. The underlying assumption here is that if the public sector would only follow the lead of the private sector most problems of governance would be over. Such an assumption is not always correct since there are some functions of government in which private sector approaches may not be applicable such as defence, national security, police etc.

In some cases, governments have faced threats to govern effectively and have consequently sought not only to become more efficient and effective but also to make policies that enable incumbent politicians to be re-elected. This explains why governments of the political right were successful electorally and sought

116

to impose radically new forms of action on the public sector. Yet, in cases where the political left remained in power, it tended to adopt many of the techniques used by the right. In the UK, for example, some of the policies and management practices introduced by Margaret Thatcher's government have been pursued by the Labour Party in power under Tony Blair.

A number of such practices are retained as good public management conceptualised as managerialism. The managerialist belief is that there is a body of sound management practice applicable to the private sector that is generic in its scope and thus, directly transferable to the private sector, subject to cultural limits.

The inculcation of managerialist values in public agencies has put pressure on civil servants to adopt business management practices on the grounds that:

- management problems related to service delivery by public agencies are complex, technical matters relating to productive efficiency, productivity and costs which are best resolved by highly technical experts;

- centrally imposed regulations and externally imposed political and policy constraints unreasonably restrain expert management decision-making;

- technical abilities and management capacities are the proper basis for establishing and maintaining the right to manage public service delivery processes, which is a move towards the de-politicisation of complex organisational and environmental issues that would otherwise be resolved within public and political forums; and

- politics and policy, therefore, are properly reduced to constraining rather than enabling forces within public service delivery agencies; thus, *ipso facto*, the adoption of private sector management practices constitutes private sector management of public agencies.[12]

In some countries, public sector executives may neither have the required expertise nor the willingness or ability to learn from the outcomes of past decisions because of the way in which they were recruited, i.e. on political grounds rather than merit. Public policies and the political process are often products of incremental adaptation to changing problems. Thus, intentions change, plans become irrelevant and consistency becomes an impediment to the day-to-day management of issues, crises and problems. In other words, the principles of consistency, continuity and precedence become the major objective instrument of solving emerging and unforeseen problems. Such principles, applied in a changing environment, can hinder rather than facilitate a change process.

The managerialist approach appears to seek to shift public agencies from an allegiance to the bureaucratic (hierarchy and control) paradigm to an acceptance of a post-bureaucratic (innovation and support) paradigm. Managerialist pressures thus create a need for a unique set of organisational changes within public agencies that would bring them into a more congruent strategic fit. This means aligning strategies, culture and leadership styles to environments. This requires public agencies to:

- become more performance-oriented, whilst maintaining organisational integrity and protecting extant professional and technical standards; and

- manage by anticipation the organisational and behavioural changes needed to achieve the desired level of performance.

In order to achieve the desired changes, a public organisation therefore has to embark on multi-faceted organisational development process involving:

- the articulation of organisational goals, embracing increased effectiveness such as better quality service;

- the specification of the likely impact of the changes on the organisation;

- the development of an implementation plan for the proposed goal or change involving all the stakeholders;

- the implementation of organisational change strategies and tactics, involving an entire organisation or a coherent part thereof; and

- the monitoring of the impact and success of the implemented change strategies in order to determine whether and when adjustments to them are needed.

The adoption of a performance orientation and strategies for a development process as discussed above has an impact on public agencies regarding the structure, culture and leadership of the organisation.

Structure

Performance orientation, for example, demands a review and perhaps a recasting of structure, i.e. its management – prescribed roles to ensure that it is aligned with performance goals and also ensuring that the required strategies for control are in place to facilitate the efficient and effective conduct of its activities. The organisational structure that is appropriate for performance orientation would have the following characteristics:

- vertically flatter, so that problem-solving decisions, especially in relation to service delivery, can be made at points that are closer to clients so as to reduce performance-sensitive, decision-response times, to simplify co-ordination and reduce communications distortions;

- less formalised, to give staff more discretion in satisfying idiosyncratic client needs; and

- horizontally more complex, even one with a significant degree of spatial differentiation, as service providers find an advantage in being geographically closer to their clients.

Cultural change

Organisational cultures, at an operational level, comprise three inter-related dimensions:

- a socio-cultural system of the perceived functioning of an organisation's strategies and practices;
- an organisational value system; and
- the collective beliefs of individuals working within the organisation.

A public agency's traditional ideals, norms and values must change if it is to inculcate a performance-oriented organisational culture that:

- supports managerialist values and attitudes;
- encourages behaviours that are performance-related;
- emphasises quality service, adaptability, creativity, initiative, cohesion and team work;
- gives employees leeway to make mistakes, but requires that they learn from them;
- recognises the diversity of commitments and affiliations that civil servants have;
- acknowledges that individual behaviours will differ according to individual beliefs about public service; risk preferences; attitude to change and tolerances of ambiguity and indeterminacy.[13]

The new culture will have its own basic assumptions, values, beliefs and visible artifacts such as dress codes and office layout.

Manager/Leadership

The successful implementation of managerialist reform requires leadership that is capable of:

- redefining organisational primary purpose and core beliefs;
- creating a vision of how the post-reform future will look in terms of organisational structure, culture and performance standard;
- defining the required strategic objectives within a medium to long-term perspective;
- planning and resourcing adequately the necessary structural and procedural changes; and
- empowering those expected to assume group leadership positions.

It should be mentioned that managerialist reform may improve the performance of public agencies, but only if a wide variety of challenges and threats confronting them can be addressed at the organisational, service delivery and policy levels. One of the challenges facing public agencies is the need to train and retrain managers so that they are clearly familiar with the rationale and process of change. In general, the managerialist approach expects public managers to improve organisational efficiency, be effective in reducing costs, and, at the same time, enhance organisational performance by meeting the often competing needs of a variety of stakeholders. This can be done within a politico-administrative environment that punishes mistakes and rewards risk-averse behaviour, regardless of the costs and effort involved in avoiding unacceptable or intolerable outcomes flowing from administrative decisions.

The public and private sector mix of management practice and processes are only a means to address management problems and issues. The mix is basically a practical approach that is not based entirely on any social theory or management theory. It is a way of finding out what works at a particular point in time in historical development processes and practices.

REFERENCES

1. Dewar, D. B., Public Service Values: How to Navigate in Rough Waters, in The Dewar Series: Perspectives on Public Management. Values in the Public Service: Canadian Centre for Management Development, June 1994, p 1.

2. Africa Recovery, United Nations Volume 9, No. 3, November 1995.

3. Agere, S., and Jorm, N., (2000) Designing Performance Appraisal Systems, Commonwealth Secretariat, London.

4. Agere, S., and Mandaza, I., (1999) Rethinking Policy Analysis. Enhancing Policy Development and Management in the Public Service. Commonwealth Secretariat, London.

5. Carnall, C., Managing Change: Self-Development for Managers. Routledge, London 1991, p 91.

6. Commonwealth Secretariat: From Problem to Solution: Commonwealth Strategies for Reform: Managing the Public Service Strategies for Improvement Series: No. 1, p 34.

7. Korac-Kakabadse A., and Korac-Kakabadse, N. Leadership in Government: Study of the Australian Public Service. Ashgate, London 1998, p 135.

8. op cit

9. The Times, Tuesday, August 24, 1999.

10. ibid

11. Guy Peters: Governance in a Changing Environment. McGill-Queens University Press, Canada.

12. Dixon, John, Kouzmin, A and Nada Korac-Kakabdse, Managerialism – Something Old, Something New. Economic Prescription versus Effective Organisational Change in Public Agencies. International Journal of Public Sector Management, Vol. II, No. 2/3, 1998.

13. ibid

TEACHING, TRAINING AND MANAGEMENT DEVELOPMENT FOR PUBLIC SERVICES

INTRODUCTION

Across the Commonwealth in states big and small, developed and developing, one clearly articulated challenge for public management relates to the development and retention of management staff. There is now great interest in many Commonwealth countries in the development of the Senior Public Service or Senior Executive. In recent times, there have been strategic reviews of the Civil Service College in the United Kingdom, the Canadian Centre for Management Development in Canada, the creation of a public service Learning Resource Centre in Trinidad and Tobago, and attempts to refocus the training of public service managers in Barbados. These and other initiatives underscore the urgency with which many public services are now treating the issue of management development.

Indeed, many who now reflect on the past decades of, at times, frenzied activity on public service reform, point to deficiencies in management skills, and recognise that sustained reform programmes demand the development and retention of appropriate management skills. Politicians and civil society are now demanding a public sector that is more service-oriented and performance-oriented. They are, in turn, willing to give public sector managers more autonomy and better tools to do the job. One of those tools must be management skill. Public sector training and management development therefore must also become more performance-oriented. Governments will need to be assured that training is producing a more capable, effective and creative public service.

In focusing on this challenge the following issues will be addressed:

- the environment of the new public service manager;
- the use of competencies to guide curriculum development and training programme delivery;
- curriculum and programme development;
- training and development methodologies; and
- appropriate institutional frameworks for the design and delivery of training.

123

THE ENVIRONMENT OF THE NEW PUBLIC ADMINISTRATION

This section provides an overview of the environment within which the new public administration operates and sketches the elements of the new public administration agenda. Training and development for the public service must develop within this context.

GLOBALISATION

We live in an increasingly global and interdependent world. On a worldwide level, globalisation may be seen to relate to the economic interdependence across countries as reflected in increasing cross-border flows of goods and services, capital and know-how. It is underpinned by developments in world organisations such as the WTO, and the growing acceptance of new principles and guidelines governing international trade. With respect to a specific country, globalisation refers to the extent of inter-linkages between the country's economy and the rest of the world. A specific company would focus on the extent to which it trades or operates across the globe.

Paradoxically, as we focus on this atmosphere of global interchange, powerful regional economic blocs are emerging, leading to the opening up of borders and heightening even greater interdependence within those regions.

Globalisation is being driven by factors, which include:

- an increasing number of countries are embracing the free market ideology;
- acceptance of the World Trade Organisation and its principles and rulings;
- technological advances, which includes, most importantly, information technology; and
- the opening of borders to trade, investment and technology transfers.

The globalisation movement has sparked many debates about its impact on people and communities and the extent to which it has led to widening gaps between rich and poor countries, and exacerbated income gaps within countries. The world has witnessed significant economic and financial fluctuations in South East Asia, Brazil and Russia. There are concerns, therefore, about the actual and potential growth in social inequalities. One element of the way forward must be greater accountability. There is the need for more dialogue between business, government and civil society. Indeed, some are now advocating the embrace by business of the triple bottom line, which would focus on financial, environmental and social accountability.

INFORMATION TECHNOLOGY

Rapid advances in information technology continue to drive significant societal and organisational changes. All sectors of civil society have moved to embrace IT advances to increase efficiency and effectiveness. Developments in IT now make it possible to assemble teams across the globe that work together without any face-to-face interaction. The power of IT to facilitate both information exchange, and financial transactions has now been firmly accepted across all sectors.

The Internet has emerged as a critical medium for commerce and information exchange, and it is being used increasingly as a vehicle to facilitate dialogue between government and civil society.

The Chief Information Officer (CIO) has now become increasingly common in both the public and private sectors. CIOs are now taking responsibility for information system strategy, setting standards and promulgating best practice in IT development and management.

There is also the issue of access to Information Technology. Wealthier countries and citizens have better access. Some governments are attempting to ensure a basic level of access for all citizens. This could include programmes in schools as well as a community-based access programme. Governments are also increasingly turning to IT to improve service delivery to citizens.

Information Technology will continue to be one of the most powerful drivers of change as we enter the new millennium.

DEMAND FOR CITIZEN AND COMMUNITY EMPOWERMENT

Technology now makes it feasible for governments to seek citizens' views on a wide range of issues, and citizens are increasingly demanding this access. Policy-making must become more inclusive. Much of the demand for citizen and community involvement in decision-making stems from concerns about the failings of modern democracy. There is an increasing concern that citizens are not just consumers or customers of public services. They also have concerns about how well they operate together in communities. They demand an involvement beyond periodically voting at an election, which is a more passive rather than an active involvement in the on-going process of governance.

We hear increasingly of concepts such as "citizen engagement" and "active citizenship". This points to the growing movement to devise new measures for citizens' participation.

One element of this concern for greater participation focuses on consultation on what governments should do – the policy debate. There is much discussion now on instruments such as deliberative polling, referenda, citizen's jury, or Internet chat lines. In addition, there is also increasing concern with how things are done – the implementation debate.

Some governments have indeed already begun to experiment with arrangements requiring collaborative planning and some degree of shared decision-making. These new collaborative partnerships are in effect new models of governance. The redefined governance practices impact on three basis relationships:

- federal and provincial governments;
- central agencies and line departments; and
- citizens and their governments.

QUESTIONING EXISTING POLITICAL/PARLIAMENTARY SYSTEMS

Another element of the demand for citizen and community involvement is the growing scepticism and cynicism with respect to existing political and parliamentary systems. There are those who now take issue with the traditional approaches to political activity.

The time has come for politics to move away from the adversarial style to finding ways for parties to work together, finding consensus rather than conflict, problem-solving rather than point-scoring, getting things done rather than merely stating one's view, looking for common ground rather than operating in tribes and acting out of vengeance and hate.

These concerns have led to increased debate about the appropriateness of different voting systems. The concerns have also raised issues about the structure and functioning of parliaments, and institutional and support mechanisms for parliamentarians.

126

The backdrop to all of this is a quest for new relations between citizens and the organisations for governance. It is really a quest for new alliance and partnership agreements.

Citizens are now increasingly demanding a system that truly reflects the diversity and pluralism of the societies in which they live, and allows all voices to be heard in every forum where decisions are made. We need to find mechanisms where we can benefit from the different skills, knowledge and expertise of others.

ECOLOGICAL CONCERNS

Ecological issues are now recognised as being among the most critical challenges of our age. All sectors of society need to address this challenge. It is at the heart of concerns about sustainable development.

In addressing these concerns, some governments are now insisting on environmental impact studies for all major investments. Environmental audits are increasingly being utilised by both private and public sector bodies.

Societal programmes focusing on the environment have also included:

- communication;
- environmental management;
- education;
- developing products and services that are environmentally friendly;
- information and education on the safe use and disposal of products;
- recycling;
- emergency plans to deal with accidents; and
- research on the impact of materials, products and processes.

These very real concerns with our environment will shape much of what we do in organisations in the future.

DIVERSITY ISSUES

Much conflict, both between nations and within countries in recent times, seems to be fuelled by intolerance and a failure to appreciate and value differences. The forces of globalisation and the growing interdependence of countries will bring into sharp focus the need to respect differences. The management of diversity therefore will be a critical challenge as we enter the new millennium.

Increasingly, private sector organisations are recognising the competitive advantage that can be gained from multinational teams. The success of the new global corporation will depend in large measure on their ability to create and manage multinational and cross-cultural teams.

Within countries as well, governments are challenged to ensure that all groups feel a sense of inclusion. Issues of race, ethnicity, gender, age, religion and sexual orientation are all elements that need careful attention and policies and practices must foster inclusion.

The issues of globalisation, information technology, citizen empowerment, quest for more appropriate political systems, diversity and ecological concerns are perhaps some of the most powerful forces impacting on our world. They are the context within which we must act. Partnering for good governance is an imperative and fits squarely within the context outlined above. Institutions in civil society have been responding to these challenges.

THE NEW PUBLIC ADMINISTRATION

Public sectors around the world need to respond to the drivers for change outlined above. In addition, many public sectors face other challenges, which include:

- economic and fiscal crisis;
- structural adjustment imperatives and conditionalities;
- need to improve national competitiveness;
- demands by citizens for improved service; and
- failings of existing public administration.

Against this background, a review of current public service reform programmes show the following as core issues on the agenda of the new public administration:

- *Rethinking and re-shaping government*
  This includes issues relating to increased citizen engagement – the challenge of new governance arrangements and strengthening policy capacity.

128

- *Repositioning organisations and managing change*
  This includes issues of managing reorganisation and strategic change.

- *Redesigning and improving service delivery*
  This includes devolving service delivery to others, the introduction of citizen charters and the use of single window or one-stop delivery systems.

- *Reframing performance measures and accountability*
  This focuses on the challenges to improve public accountability and the development of new frameworks for performance management.

- *Revitalising human resource capacity and organisational performance*
  This includes the development of competency profiles, a renewed focus on the development of a senior civil service, and focused approaches on training and development.

- *Renewing management and organisation system*
  Included in this agenda item are issues relating to increased utilisation of information technology, and the introduction of new financial management systems.

- *Revisiting stakeholder relationships*
  This focuses on issues such as new partnering arrangements, and political/administrative interface.

In addition to this reform agenda, many public services are beginning to envision themselves as borderless learning organisations demonstrating effective leadership. The issue of "borderlessness" has also been characterised in the United Kingdom as "joined-up" government. This speaks to the need to break down the "silos", which very often characterise public service organisations. This relates to both policy formulation and service delivery. In creating the borderless organisation, public service managers will need to ensure that there is widespread sharing of information, and the delegation and sharing of authority.

The public service, as a learning organisation, will require a culture characterised by:

- reflecting on and rationalising experience, turning individual learning into organisational expertise;
- co-ordinating the results of studies, giving insights into best practice, and disseminating the results;

- rewarding the process of learning; and
- adding to and keeping up to date the intellectual capital available through research and study.

This is the environment and vision of the new public administration, which must inform training and development initiatives. One approach to translating this environment and vision to a training framework is through the development of competency profiles.

USING COMPETENCY-BASED HRD APPROACHES

Many public services have begun to use competency-based human resource management approaches. This competency approach would facilitate the introduction of more effective, valid and useful criteria for the recruitment, succession management and personal and career planning of senior managers. It therefore provides a basis on which training and development programmes could be developed and instituted. The competency approach focuses on the issue of the content of training.

Competency is generally seen to refer to the set of behavioural patterns an incumbent needs to bring to the position to perform the task and functions with competence. Competencies are underpinned by specific skills, specialised knowledge demands and attributes that are considered to be important in performing task to required standards. A distinction also needs to be made between "core" competencies and "technical" or "specialist" competencies. The "technical" or "specialist" competencies are those that are critical to the specific areas of a department's endeavours. This section focuses on "core" competencies. There are a variety of approaches that may be used to identify required competencies. This discussion draws on the articulated competencies from a number of Commonwealth countries including Australia, Barbados, Canada, New Zealand and the United Kingdom. An examination of them shows very clearly that they are linked to the current environment and challenges impacting on the contemporary public sector.

The following competencies seem critical given the environmental challenges outlined above:

- ***Building and Sustaining Relationships***
  Concerned with establishing and maintaining positive working relationships with people at all levels within the public and private sectors, related industry

130

and community interest groups, and wider national and international communities.

- ***Commitment to Achievement***
  Concerned with a personal commitment to excellence and a focus on attaining organisational goals and objectives. An action orientation that ensures a focus on short- and long-term consequences of strategies.

- ***Effective Communication***
  Concerned with clear and effective two-way communication with a wide range of people and in all situations. This includes the ability to listen and therefore to provide an opportunity for others to have input.

- ***Honesty and Integrity***
  Concerned with modelling the highest standards of personal, professional and institutional behaviour and helping to ensure a politically impartial and incorrupt public service.

- ***Intellectual Capability***
  Concerned with the capacity to understand and respond strategically to the complexities inherent in service to the public.

- ***Learner***
  Concerned with the willingness and ability to be open to new ideas and concepts and committed to continuous learning.

- ***Management of Transformation***
  Concerned with an understanding of managing complex system change.

- ***Managing in the Political Cultural Context***
  Concerned with having the ability to understand the conventions, structure, functions and objectives of government and the wider cultural, economic and social environment in which it operates, and positioning the department accordingly.

- ***Personal Mastery***
  Concerned with having an appropriate sense of self, self-confidence, and the ability to maintain high energy, stability, stamina and values.

- *Strategic Leadership*
  Concerned with forward thinking, seeking and accepting challenges and opportunities and developing and communicating a clear, inspiring and relevant direction for the department.

These competencies provide a foundation for many human resource management initiatives, including training and development.

TOWARDS CURRICULUM AND PROGRAMME DEVELOPMENT

Curriculum and programmes must facilitate the development of managers, capable of leading public service organisations which:

- Focus on outcomes with an emphasis on people's needs and their convenience rather than administrative processes and structures, giving effective service to the public.

- Move beyond 'efficiency in silos' to high quality, outcome-focused strategic thinking. This must involve anticipating problems, networking and partnering.

- Focus on service delivery partnerships with other parts of the civil service, using the power of IT and allowing a positive management of risk.

The training and development agenda would therefore need to include the following elements:

- management of effective service delivery to the public;
- the development of quality policy advice;
- high quality, outcome-oriented strategic thinking;
- effectiveness in communication, including communication with the media;
- effective handling of global dimensions to policy-making;
- management skills which include:
  - developing, tasking and motivating teams and individuals
  - focusing on outcomes and effectiveness while retaining propriety and efficiency
  - organisation and management development
  - change management
  - project management;

- financial management and assessment of value for money;
- leadership skills;
- diversity management;
- ethics, values and principles of the public sector;
- mentoring and coaching skills;
- emotional intelligence.

The development of the programme must also focus on the identification of the critical core to be exposed to management development programmes. Training and development must be service-wide, and there is therefore a need for well-structured activities, from induction and appropriately phased programmes through all levels in the public service.

The Canadian Public Service has developed a management trainees' programme. Trainees are selected from either recent Master's degree graduates or junior officers in the public service. The programme is of four years' duration. Job assignments include rotations in regional offices, central agencies and line departments. Training activities include site visits, case studies, small group exercises and personal learning plans, with a focus on experiential work.

In India, there is a particular focus on the Indian Administrative Service, which is a group of 6,000 career officers who hold the most senior-appointed positions in district, state and national government. Each year, a group of fewer than 100 officers is chosen for focused management development activity. Their initial training is a two-year induction course involving academic and language training. A substantial component of the training is experiential, involving placements in a district government, a large public sector organisation or NGO. Throughout their careers there are planned and phased refresher courses which, among other things, focus on policy development, information technology and human resource management.

Much of Singapore's training for the senior public service focuses on preparing for the future. This concentrates on three themes:

- Welcoming change;
- Anticipating change; and
- Implementing change.

The Singapore Public Service has also established a target of 100 hours of training per year, and has directed supervisors to meet annually, with each supervisor laying out and then revising a training road map. Members of the administrative service receive several months of induction training, including a two-week study trip to other capitals. They also have postings to private sector firms, unions or NGOs. After three or four years, they attend a compulsory one-week programme focusing on supervisory skills. Deputy secretaries are required to take a four-week programme on policy development that emphasises identifying and testing the assumptions underlying particular policies and anticipating the impact of policies. Training continues at the senior level, with deputy secretaries taking advanced management programmes overseas and permanent secretaries going on sabbaticals at universities or research institutions.

The Canadian Centre for Management Development has also introduced a corporate leadership programme. This programme has the following five modules:

- leadership renewal;
- leadership and learning, with an emphasis on coaching;
- service quality;
- co-ordinated policy development; and
- continuous learning.

Each module is one week or less in duration and the entire programme extends over a period of 18 months to two years. There are assignments between modules, as well as meetings with coaches and mentors, and assessments.

Curriculum and programme development must be firmly embedded in sound strategic human resource management and development frameworks. This framework must include appropriate recruitment and selection, sound performance management and appraisal, and career counselling and planning. The framework acknowledges the desirability of identifying 'high flyers' and providing fast-track mechanisms for their movement to the top of the public service organisation.

Curriculum and programme development must also be results-focused. All too often training and development activity may transfer some knowledge, but may not help trainers learn how to get desired results. The information and tools may have been transferred to make the participants better people, but not to help them achieve better performance. As the public service generally is becoming more performance-oriented, training and development must also become more performance-oriented.

It is also clear that training methodology is critical. Much adult learning happens on the job. For training to be successful it must be linked closely to work. Ideally, modules should be short but the learning programmes should be continuous. Experiential methodology is critical; coaching and mentoring are important components.

TRAINING AND DEVELOPMENT METHODOLOGIES

Public services are now utilising a range of approaches to ensure effective delivery of training and development. Workshops, courses and structural activities have their place in leadership and management development. Experiential methodology, however, has clearly been demonstrated to be the most effective. This section outlines some of the methodologies in use in the public service environment.

Job assignments

Well-selected, planned and focused job assignments can be an extremely valuable development tool. These assignments can be inside or outside the public services and inside or outside the country. An earlier section indicated an approach that provided an opportunity for public officers to be attached to NGOs and private sector organisations. In utilising this approach, a clear link must be established between the assignment and a development need or competency requirement. Public officers must see the assignment in the context of their career path and the organisation's goals.

Mentoring

Mentoring may be seen as a relationship between two individuals based on a mutual desire for development towards an organisational objective. The relationship is a non-reporting one. Mentoring generally benefits the mentor, the mentoree and others in the wider organisation. This is where mentoring and the learning organisation are linked very powerfully. There are three aspects of learning:

- the learning of the mentor and how this affects their impact on the organisation;
- the learning of the mentoree and the impact on the organisation; and
- how the organisation proactively promotes the processors of sharing learning.

135

As part of the process of being a mentor, individuals should be encouraged to examine their own management style. Mentorees often learn how to pause and take time to reflect on what they are doing and this produces improvements in management. Public services can therefore use mentoring to stimulate organisational learning, and as an important intervention in the training and development process.

Coaching

Coaching and mentoring are very often lumped together in discussions on training and development. Coaching may be distinguished from mentoring and seen as more directive and focused on the job. It is a process often carried out by line managers. Mentoring is a non-directive relationship and generally more broadly focused. The mentor usually takes the longer perspective for both the individual and the organisation. A facilitative style is appropriate for both mentoring and coaching. Mentors can act in a coaching capacity as part of the mentoring relationship. It is, however, quite possible for mentoring to take place with no element of coaching. This is why valuable mentors do not have to be knowledgeable in the specialisms of the mentoree. However, if a specific competency needs to be developed in a mentoree, then it may be a conscious decision to link that mentoree with a mentor who majors in that competency.

Coaching, however, may be seen as being more directly linked to performance issues, and is part of the overall responsibility of line management. It is an important ingredient in the mix of approaches to training and development.

FORMAL TRAINING PROGRAMMES

Public services would also continue to rely on a range of formal training programmes of varying lengths. These could include degree and diploma programmes, workshops, seminars etc. It would be critical to match the development needs of individuals with the objectives and orientation of the particular programme. Programmes must be designed with the competency needs of the trainers as the primary focus. Training programmes, therefore, must be demand-driven and results-focused.

Being results-focused would require that every module or workshop begin and end with explicit statements of the intended results for the organisation of the skill being taught. Evaluation of training programmes therefore should focus on how participants feel their learning experiences will impact on organisation results.

Many formal training programmes would also provide opportunities for participants to complete research projects, which could also facilitate the linkage between the training and intended organisation results.

PERFORMANCE APPRAISAL

Performance appraisal is a developmental tool and provides a mechanism for appraisers and appraisees to establish mutually agreed performance targets against which to measure achievement. The appraisal process also provides a context for feedback about demonstrated competence on the job. The appraisal process also provides the opportunity for the development and review of training plans for appraisees.

Performance appraisal needs to be seen, therefore, not as a once-a-year, form-filling activity, but as an on-going process of dialogue and feedback about performance and behaviours against targets and expectations. Used in this way, it becomes an integral part of the training and development process of the public service.

In general, it must be stressed that training approaches must use adult learning pedagogy. Increasingly in training institutions there is a clear linkage of training to practice, with student involvement shaping assessment practices and programme design. The training environment also needs to provide a safe space to facilitate critical thinking and the exploration of issues in a confidential manner.

INSTITUTIONAL ROLES

Within countries there are many institutions involved in the process of public service training and development. This section overviews the major institutions, their views and contributions.

Ministries and departments

In most countries, the responsibility for training is located in ministries or departments. These units must therefore develop training plans, and determine the appropriate service provider. The human resource management systems within departments therefore need to be in place to facilitate this role, and line managers need to be aware of their human resource management responsibilities in this regard.

Some departments may have their own training function and may be able to satisfy some of their training needs. These training units would need to maintain linkages with other training institutions to ensure dovetailing of programmes, and consistency with respect to overall philosophy.

Public Service colleges and research institutions

Many Commonwealth countries have been reviewing the role and structure of their public service colleges in light of environmental changes, and the evolving challenges of the new public administration. In the United Kingdom for instance, a review of the Civil Service College concluded that the college had done well in providing middle management training, and had survived in a competitive environment with no central subsidies. This was in the context of departments being free to purchase training from the universities and the private sector. The College, however, was perceived as being less effective at addressing strategic, organisational development and senior leadership issues. As a consequence of this, the Government has incorporated the Civil Service College into a newly established Centre for Management and Policy Studies in the Cabinet Office. While the Civil Service College will continue to provide a variety of programmes for middle management, the new Centre will be responsible for strategic core programmes for the senior civil service, such as the Top Management Programme. There will also be a research budget to facilitate research on key issues.

The Canadian Centre for Management Development also has a research division which is responsible for research projects. This Centre offers two types of programmes: career development programmes aimed at selected individuals within both the executive group and executive feeder groups, and corporate learning programmes with wider enrolment from across the entire public service. Both sets of programmes are congruent with a list of competencies that the public service has identified for all its executives.

One debate continuing in many countries relates to funding for management training. One option is for the department to pay on a per-person, per-course basis or for the programme to be financed centrally. The virtue of the former is that it forces a department seriously to consider whether it is getting value for money. When programmes are intended for people viewed as a corporate resource for the public service, central financing is more likely.

Universities

Universities provide an important external resource for public sector training. Many universities have now moved to develop programmes specifically geared to public service managers. The Centre for Management Development in Barbados, which is an autonomous body within the University of the West Indies delivering graduate and executive programmes, has recently launched an MBA for public service managers. This programme is intended to help public sector managers become more quantitative, analytical and strategic in their approach. It makes extensive use of case studies as well as project and group work. Many other universities have developed programmes for public service managers with business schools.

The traditional public administration programmes in universities have tended to be located in social sciences or political science departments. These departments have typically been very slow in responding to the changing dynamics of the new public administration. Indeed in the 1980s and early 1990s, many academics were highly critical of developments in the new public administration. This reluctance on the part of traditional public administration academics, coupled with the demand for more management skills by public service managers led to business schools taking the lead in many university programmes geared to the new public administration.

In addition, many university academics have not embraced the principles and practices of adult training methodologies. Many continue to feel more comfortable in the traditional lecturing mode. This has also adversely affected the contributions which universities have been able to make in the area of executive development.

Other institutions

There are private sector and NGO institutions providing executive development programmes. It is absolutely necessary that executives from the public sector participate in programmes with private sector and NGO executives. This facilitates the partnering that must take place across these sectors. It must also mean that public service executive programmes should be open to private sector and NGO executives. Whatever the institution, evaluations must ensure that they provide value for money.

It is also becoming clear that programmes need to be developed for ministers and the political directorate. In many countries, seminars and team-building exercises for ministers are now regular features. One of the critical issues on the new public administration agenda is the political/administrative interface. Training and development programmes are an intervention that can facilitate the improvement of the interface. In general, there is now recognition of the value of training for politicians, as well as an interest in finding ways of providing it that will be effective and respectful of traditional lines of accountability.

TOWARDS THE FUTURE

Change and continuous learning will continue to characterise public services in the future. The realisation of the public service as a borderless learning organisation necessitates the embrace of the principles and values of learning by the public service.

The public service will also need to ensure that its training and development is truly results-focused. On-going and systematic evaluation must therefore also be performance-focused.

The on-going reforms of the public service will require a proactive commitment to reform. The effectiveness of the public service will depend on the leadership skills and knowledge of public service staff. Planned and dedicated training and development must therefore become firmly embedded in public services.

CONCLUSION

In the past, the teaching of public administration in universities has tended to focus on theoretical perspectives of government and its institutions, with minimum reference to practical issues prevailing in society at any one point in time. The argument posed here is that while teaching government is good for undergraduates, the curriculum should now be extended to cover contemporary issues which generally constitute major elements of good governance. Such elements include, for example, the rule of law, freedom of expression and association, electoral legitimacy, accountability and transparency and development-oriented leadership. These elements constitute major links and bridges between theory and practice.

It has also been argued that while it is appropriate to provide good grounding in theories on the role of the state, society and institutions, attempts must now be made to incorporate into undergraduate courses contemporary issues in good governance. The emphasis should be based on achieving the results that answer the questions and needs of society and solve some of the problems often experienced in the process of maintaining good governance. In addition to the role of the state, some of the contemporary issues have included the nature, type and structure of sub-national governments, local government institutions, public enterprises, autonomous government agencies, administrative tribunals and other *ad hoc* agencies set up by government from time to time, depending on the nature of the problem to be addressed.

The teaching of good governance is therefore advocated as an extension to what is already provided by the current system or courses. The need for such an extension is based on the desire to be socially inclusive of the contemporary issues emerging in society.

Training, as used in this context, generally refers to the acquisition of skills, knowledge and information by those who occupy positions in the state, organisations and institutions. It aims to equip practitioners with the skills to enable them to improve their performance and, ultimately, the delivery of service to society. Training in these circumstances must be continuous, relevant and responsive to emerging trends and issues. The challenge is not only the acquisition of relevant skills in a particular discipline or occupation, but also to those who impart and deliver the skills. They must also upgrade their skills and understanding of the complex issues that they are called upon to address.

Training is therefore regarded as an enabling instrument with which to develop a capacity to grapple with the emerging trends, principles and perspectives of management often drawn from practical experience.

Management development as used here refers to the upgrading, advancing and improving of the skills and knowledge base of those practitioners who manage human, financial and material resources. In order to meet the emerging issues, management is now expected to widen its role and also find ways of involving the stakeholders. In order to respond to the dynamic changes experienced in managing resources, managers are expected to improve their skills and knowledge base, particularly in the delivery of services to the public. Innovative strategies to improve the delivery of service to the public have been identified and continue to be modified to suit the ever-changing development agenda. Many advances have been made through creative and critical thinking and sharing globally ideas in management. Such advances in the organisation and creation of knowledge have been observed in, for example, decision-making, delegation, strategic planning, organisational development and design and the controlling function. In particular, managing people, work groups, leading people in organisation, financial and human resources management and, above all, communication and negotiation aspects of management, have been improved in the last decade. Traditional approaches, while essential, are being replaced by the demands for modernisation and by the new public management paradigm that has already been discussed.

One of the biggest challenges facing managers is the management of change, pressure for change, strategic planning for change, organising both political and economic change and managing the entire change process. Because of these different pressures for change, managers are now expected to be involved in policy development, policy management and the evaluation of their policy implementation processes. As new initiatives in policy development and policy management are tried regularly in the management of resources, managers need to keep themselves well informed of the various innovations. This implies that training institutions should have the requisite skills, resources and knowledge to impart to practitioners.

In an attempt to make teaching, training and management in good governance more effective and sustainable to practitioners, experience has shown that ethics and values play an important role. Ethics, as commonly understood, refers to principles of behaviour that distinguish between good, bad, right and wrong. The purpose of ethics or a code of ethics is to enable individuals to make choices from a number of alternative behaviours. The importance of ethics increases in proportion to the consequences of the outcome of a behaviour. As an individual's actions become more consequential for others, the ethics of that individual become more important.

The role and state of ethics in business have become a growing concern among managers and the public. Several factors have contributed to this phenomenon. First, scandals involving unethical activities by several major corporations are being widely publicised. Secondly, business ethics have become a topic of concern because businesses are realising that ethical misconduct by management can be extremely costly for the company and for society as a whole. Thirdly, both managers and the public are realising that the dynamics of ethics in management decision-making are often a complex and challenging phenomenon, and that determining what is and what is not ethical is often difficult to do.

Managers must reconcile competing values in making decisions. They make decisions that have consequences for themselves, the organisation that employs them and the society in which they and the organisation exist. In general, a manager's decisions affect people's lives and well-being, determine "fair" resource allocation and implement and interpret organisational rules and policies.

Ethics and codes of conduct are critically important in that they underpin the whole management of resources and the delivery of service to the public. Because of their importance, management training must include ethics in their training programme and courses. The code of ethics or code of conduct is also being applied to politicians, ministers, public servants and those who deliver public goods and services such as the professionals in medicine, health, education, social work, law etc. Since management is becoming more and more complex, it is necessary that managers and trainers acquire the relevant knowledge and skills of the role of ethical conduct in delivery of public services.

The concept of good governance, as argued here, includes more than public administration and the relationships, methods and instruments of governing. It encompasses the set of relationships between government and citizens, acting as both individuals and as part of or through institutions, for example, political parties, productive enterprises, special interest groups and the media.

It would appear from this debate and from studies that have been conducted, that the success of promoting and sustaining good governance, depends upon a number of factors, which include: conducive political and economic environment; an efficient and effective public service; vibrant public and private sector interface; an active civil society and, more importantly, the interaction between and among these institutions and organisations.

The central challenges to government administration today are not only about how governments should best perform their traditional tasks, but also about what they should devolve to others to do on their behalf. Coupled with this change is the capacity of the decision-making mechanisms to keep pace with the changing nature of the demands on governments and to maintain policy coherence in a more devolved system of policy implementation. For these reasons, teaching, training and management development institutions should extend their programmes and courses to include broader issues of governance, as well as the traditional issues of public administration.

143

It is hoped that the issues raised in this book will trigger further debate on how to sharpen and focus attention on the major factors that constitute good governance. The Chinese have a saying that states: "Every journey begins with a small step". This debate, therefore, can be considered to be a small step in a long journey to the successful promotion and sustainability of good governance.

REFERENCES

CAPAM High Level Seminar for Cabinet Secretaries, Report by Sandford Borins, September 1997.

Commonwealth Secretariat (1995), Current Good Practices and New Developments in Public Service Management: A Profile of the Public Service of Canada. The Public Service Profile Series No. 1.

Commonwealth Secretariat (1995), Current Good Practices and New Developments in Public Service Management: A Profile of the Public Service of Trinidad and Tobago. The Public Service Profile Series No. 4.

Commonwealth Secretariat (1995) ibid. A Profile of the Public Service of Singapore. The Public Services Profile Series No. 8.

Donnelly, J., Gibson, J., and Ivancevich, J., (1995) Fundamentals of Management, 9th Edition. Irwin, Publishers, Boston, USA.

Commonwealth Association of Public Administration and Management (CAPAM): Government in Transition: The inaugural conference of Commonwealth Association for Public Administration and Management. Charlottetown, Prince Edward Island, Canada, 28–31 August 1994.

Agere, S., (1999) Strengthening Management Development Institutions: The Role of Management Development Institutions in Public Service Reform. Managing the Public Service: Strategies for Improvement Series: No 9, Commonwealth Secretariat.

Commonwealth Innovations: The Newsletter of the Commonwealth Association for Public Administration and Management (CAPAM) Vol 5, No. 1, 1999.

Printed in the United Kingdom
by Lightning Source UK Ltd.
92903